BOOM!

♡

-Sayman

ABM
is B2B.

PRAISE FOR *ABM IS B2B.*

"What struck me most throughout ABM is B2B was the recurring theme of unity: unity between sales and marketing, between strategy and tactics; between measurement and goals. This principle is smart, accurate and transformative, and comes at a time when it's deeply needed in the industry. And that's just the tip of the iceberg of what's contained in these pages."

— *MEAGAN EISENBERG, Chief Marketing Officer at TripActions*

"Whether you look at it as ABM, B2B, or even H2H, marketing's proper evolution is now clear. If you want to get off the 'leads' treadmill and start building real relationships and revenue, get new language, better metrics, smart frameworks, and illustrative case studies in this transformational book."

— *ETHAN BEUTE, BombBomb, VP of Marketing*

"The power of marketing technology for B2B has exploded in recent years. However, there is a danger, because the more technology you implement, the less personal marketing can become. ABM, as outlined in this book, is a way to implement modern marketing tools while still treating each interaction on a personal level."

— *DAVID MEERMAN SCOTT, Marketing strategist, entrepreneur, and bestselling author of ten books, including The New Rules of Marketing and PR*

"This is a book that should be required reading for anybody in marketing (and sales), and certainly for the C-Suite. This is just not a good read, it is a guidebook on how to adopt and implement ABM and see results. With these real-life examples, worksheets, and methodologies, any B2B organization looking to move to an ABM approach is doing themselves a disservice if they do not make this book core to their planning and strategy development."

— *CARLOS HIDALGO, CEO, VisumCx*

"This book is the playbook on how to take a programmatic approach to B2B marketing. ABM is B2B marketing, and this book shows how marketing, sales, and customer success can work together to target the right customers faster, ultimately driving impact to the bottom line."

— *OMAR AL-SINJARI, McKesson, RelayHealth Senior Manager, Digital Marketing*

"With over 90% conversion rate, ABM is clearly a no brainer when you are looking at improving pipeline and increasing engagement. With actual case studies & graphical representation of the ABM Maturity curve, Sangram's "ABM is B2B." will help kickstart a mindset shift for companies that are on the fence for ABM. The TEAM framework helps marketers build a roadmap of all the essentials for a successful ABM program. Last but not least the Episodes give you great insights into the hits and misses of companies that have ABM as a solid B2B strategy."

— *TRISH AGARWAL, Owner, Vsynergize*

"The switch to ABM marketing can be overwhelming! The book shows us a fresh way to practically implement a transformed B2B strategy that improves outcomes and streamlines your marketing model, cutting through the numerous tactics and tools that can cloud your path to success."

— *JEREMY MIDDLETON, Pramata, Sr. Dir. Digital Marketing & Revenue Ops*

"I was all-in on this book when I saw there was an entire section on 'Make your customers heroes.' From my perspective, this honest and human focus on customers in marketing and sales is still missing from a lot of leaders' strategies, especially in the B2B world, and it's hurting them. This book gives us all a roadmap to tap into the power of *ABM is B2B*. while building authentic relationships with customers, winning loyalty, and, of course, growing earnestly."

— *NICK MEHTA, Chief Executive Officer, Gainsight*

"As any B2B marketer would tell you, cutting through the noise is challenging. The same holds true for marketers seeking new resources–the sheer number of courses, certifications, and industry books is overwhelming. This is, by far, the most actionable book on ABM I've read. Sangram leaves no stone unturned for B2B marketers and sales leaders looking to scale a business. It's written by a category leader who lives and breathes what he recommends. I can think of no better ABM resource."

— *TIM KOPP, Managing Director, Hyde Park Venture Partners*

"Sangram is a brilliant pioneer of modern account-based marketing. The practices and examples he describes here give you the playbook for winning in B2B. Worth reading at least twice."

— *SCOTT BRINKER, VP Platform Ecosystem at HubSpot;*
Editor at chiefmartec.com; Program Chair of MarTech

"As a CMO, I have worked with some of the best CEOs in business today. The truly great ones realized that they modeled how the brand would be understood and what the company stood for. They were intimately involved, not only in co-creating the brand, but in living it out very publicly. They understood that the buck started and stopped with them in this extremely important area of what former Honeywell CEO Dave Cote once called 'identity in action.' This is not just about brand – it is the very essence of leadership."

— *MARK STOUSE, ROI Analytics Software CEO, MegaValue.Live Host,*
Innovator of the Year, 2x Top 25 Innovator, Fortune 100 CMO / CCO

"We are witnessing a major shift in B2B sales and marketing. *ABM is B2B.* will bridge the gap from the old to the new."

— *MICHAEL ROSE, Author, ROE Powers ROI and Founder at Mojo Media Labs*

"After reading both books back to back, I walked away from the experience thinking about book 1 as the practitioner's field guide. Book 1 gives you a lot of actionable insight into building and executing as you transform your lead generation into ABM. In fact, two years into my own ABM journey, I walked away from book 1 with an action item list that was 19 items long. Whereas book 2 feels like the visionary's narrative on why ABM. This is different from what you may have heard three years ago at choose-your-tech conference, because the fabric of this narrative is woven with real stories, real examples, and real results. The field now has many years of widely varied experience to pull from that can say, for itself: Here is what ABM is and why it matters. Book 2 takes the author's personable, relatable communication style and blends it with real-life, in-the-trenches stories, all while shifting as much focus as possible onto the leading practitioners in the field today. Book 2 gives the framework to build a common understanding across the business. Both books are huge, and both are incredibly valuable. As counterintuitive as it seems, I'd almost recommend book 2 first, and then book 1. But do yourself a favor and read them both."

— *DANIEL ENGLEBRETSON, Director, Integrated Marketing*

"This book will breathe new life and provide much-needed perspective into your B2B business development efforts."

NIKOLE ROSE, President & COO at Mojo Media Labs

"I love that the title of this book is *ABM is B2B,* and I'd go so far as to say that Sangram himself is ABM. The depth of insight he provides into the challenges, rewards, and transformation that come with ABM are second to none. He understands technology in a major way, but he also understands how strategy and people come first—and that's huge. You don't want to miss this."

— *JILL ROWLEY, Partner at Stage 2 Capital*

"I have built a career in sales consulting, and loved every minute of it. Sangram and I share many beliefs, but the one that resonates throughout this book is the concept of OneTeam. Having sales and marketing on the same page is a critical success factor, but never more so than in an account-based revenue strategy."

— *TRISH BERTUZZI, Founder & CEO at The Bridge Group*

"ABM is B2B is incisive— a must-read for ABM leaders and neophytes alike. This book offers a poignant view on the abysmal state of traditional B2B marketing, and how account-based marketing practitioners are literally flipping traditional strategies to deliver unbelievable results. Most importantly, this book delivers real-world case studies, and, more importantly, a framework that can be implemented regardless of ABM maturity or funding."

— *MALACHI THREADGILL, Masergy, Director of Demand Generation at Masergy*

"Building an account-based revenue organization is a labor of love. This book details everything, from the new common language and lexicon of ABM to building the team to aligning with others in the revenue organization and reframing how success is measured. *ABM is B2B.* prepares marketers to be the leaders of account-based transformation in their organization."

— *ERIC MARTIN, SalesLoft, Sr. Director, Demand Generation*

"Finally, a book that recognizes the critical truth that ABM is B2B. Sangram brings his trademark charm to guide readers on their evolution from ABM experimentation into mainstream adoption in this how-to guide full of important advice and examples."

— *SAMANTHA STONE, Founder, the Marketing Advisory Network. She's a fast-growth, revenue catalyst, researcher, speaker, and consultant*

"This book imparts a transformative message for business leaders and marketers alike to help their companies win. Now is the time to operate with an ABM focus to drive marketing that nets substantial results."

— *JILLIAN GARTNER, Director of ABM, Thomson Reuters*

"My first career was spent making plays on the football field, and my second career has been spent making plays in business and sales. Through both, the importance of teamwork and accountability has been utterly undeniable. *ABM is B2B.* got me fired up because Sangram hits the nail on the head in both of these areas. Marketers, salespeople, and executives alike will get a world of new perspectives by diving into this book. It's a must-read."

— *REGGIE RIVERS, former Denver Bronco, Media Personality, Benefit Auctioneer, Motivational Speaker, Master of Ceremonies, and Author*

ABM
is B2B.

Why B2B Marketing and Sales is Broken and How to Fix it

SANGRAM VAJRE

ERIC SPETT

IDEAPRESS
PUBLISHING

Copyright © 2019 by Sangram Vajre & Eric Spett

All rights reserved.

Published in the United States by Ideapress Publishing.

Ideapress Publishing | www.ideapresspublishing.com

All trademarks are the property of their respective companies.

Cover Design by Shannel Wheeler

Cataloging-in-Publication Data is on file with the Library of Congress.
ISBN: 978-1-940858951

Proudly Printed in the usa

Special Sales

Ideapress Books are available at a special discount for bulk purchases, for sales promotions and premiums, or for use in corporate training programs. Special editions, including personalized covers, a custom foreword, corporate imprints, and bonus content are also available.

We didn't write this book for ourselves. We wrote it for others who dream big and use their entrepreneurial spirit to make the world a better place. That's why all proceeds from this book are going to support New Story, an organization that is literally building a new life for thousands of people in North and Central America.

TABLE OF CONTENTS

SECTION 4: YOU CAN START TODAY BY PUTTING THE TEAM FRAMEWORK INTO ACTION

SECTION 5: FROM BORING TO BORING TO BONUS 2 BONUS

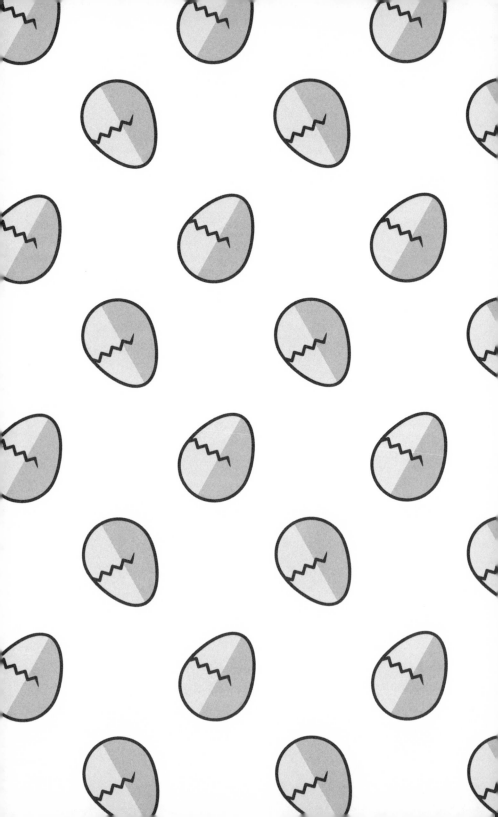

INTRODUCTION

Why Most B2B Marketing Sucks!

If you picked up this book expecting to learn what Account-Based Marketing (ABM) is, why you should do it, and why everyone is talking about it these days, we have some bad news for you. We're beyond that. The ship has sailed and you're on it, whether you know it or not. We want to help you navigate the waters properly based on your business goals. There's no debate about if with ABM—this book is focused on how.

This book is titled *ABM Is B2B*. It's not *ABM Can Help You Do B2B Better*. It's not *ABM Is the New B2B Trend to Look out for*. It's not *Do ABM Now, Do B2B Later*. We're not here to mess around with soft introductions or offer suggestions. We're here to make declarations and write new equations. Our favorite is ABM = B2B.

Here's our proof: Account-Based Marketing is an organizational strategy designed specifically to create more revenue. Business-to-Business Marketing (B2B) is an organizational strategy designed specifically to create more revenue. **Yes, they are the same.**

You can't be a successful B2B organization in today's world (no matter what the date is today, whenever you're reading this) without going after the right customers, creating experiences designed just for them, and turning them into advocates for your product or service. That is the essence of B2B marketing, and from the highest of views, it's not rocket science. The philosophy behind it is pure and makes perfect sense, yet B2B marketers have found all sorts of ways to screw it up through the years.

John Wanamaker, founder of one of the first department stores in the United States, said in the 1800s: "Half the money I spend on marketing is wasted; the trouble is I don't know which half." It was true then, and it's still true now. Ask a CEO to pinpoint what works and what doesn't in marketing, and they most likely can't tell you.

Marketing research firm Forrester discovered that fewer than one percent of all leads turn into customers. Put that another way: 99% of what you're doing now doesn't work. It's not turning into revenue. Your CEO and CFO are looking at marketing and wondering what is going on, and no one is sure what to say except that leads are coming in, and website clicks are up.

Even Seth Godin, author of 18 books and a New York Times best-seller, said this in Episode 316 of the FlipMyFunnel podcast: "It's very easy for us to think we live in this mass-market world, but we don't. We live in a micro-market world."

It's clear that B2B marketers have accepted the idea that B2B stands for **boring to boring.** We look at Apple and Uber and think, "Wow, that's groundbreaking creative work paired with amazing customer experience. How awesome is it that B2C companies get to do these cool things? Too bad I'm a B2B marketer :("

We officially declare the B2B pity party over. You are no longer bound to data sheets, stale product-demo videos, and

> **It's very easy for us to think we live in this mass-market world, but we don't. We live in a micro-market world.**

> **It's clear that B2B marketers have accepted the idea that B2B stands for boring to boring.**

way-too-long case studies as your main marketing go-tos. B2B doesn't have to suck, and this book is going to prove it. We have examples of companies creating phenomenal one-to-one experiences that customers fall in love with. Since ABM is B2B, once you start targeting the right accounts, engaging them in meaningful ways, and measuring your success, you'll have customers loving you, too.

There's a fundamental problem in B2B marketing, and ABM has presented itself as the fix. We know because we wrote the first book on it. Even then, we were doing what many marketing gurus have attempted to do since: Fit ABM into B2B, as if it were unique and different. We even flipped the funnel and created a new industry around ABM, complete with a top-50 daily business podcast called FlipMyFunnel, more than 10 conferences with thousands of attendees, and countless converts along the way.

The conversation around Account-Based Marketing has swelled in the years since our first book, and it's been amazing. But we're done with baby steps. Improving incrementally isn't the goal; growing exponentially and challenging the industry's assumptions is. It's not enough to try to persuade you that ABM is right. We have to inspire you to evolve into a marketer who cares deeply about business outcomes and is excited to rethink the value of your profession.

As you read this book, you'll notice that we use ABM and B2B interchangeably, and that's if we even mention ABM at all. That's by design, and that's how we want you to think about marketing every day. We want you to train yourself and your teams to adopt an account-based mindset and let it worm its way into your entire operation until it becomes, for lack of a better phrase, just how you do things. It's time to challenge the status quo!

ABM is transformative—the kind of change we haven't experienced in more than a decade—because it's about much more than the strategies and tactics within it. ABM is B2B. There's no separating the two.

ABM is transformative

The ABM = B2B equation blew our minds when we realized what we had, but it's not the only lesson we've learned since we wrote our first book. Because we've experienced firsthand the power of what's possible with B2B, we can look back and reflect on our own growth, our customers' successes, and our whole industry's evolution. In keeping our promise to make statements that will shatter your marketing malaise, we've discovered seven B2B truths that might shake you to your core, make you question things in a new way, and even make you mad at us for a minute. That's okay, because you'll come around. If it's really true that ABM equals B2B (and it is), can anything else be so unbelievable?

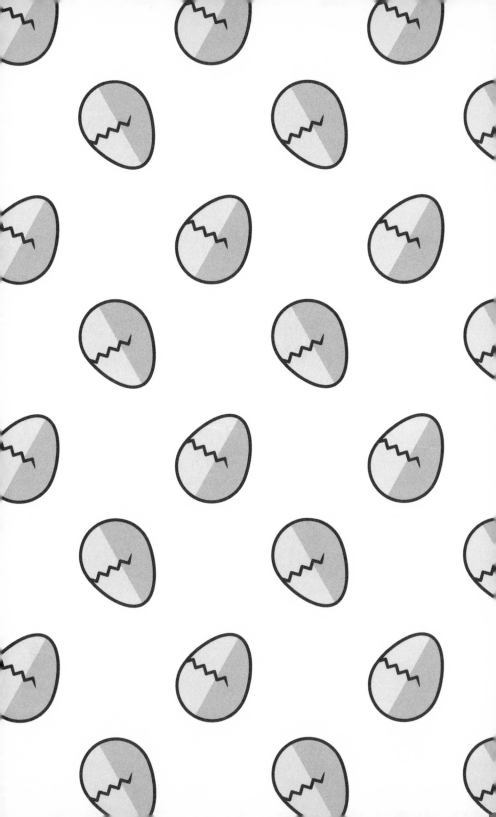

7 MARKETING AND SALES TRUTHS

THAT WILL MAKE YOUR HEAD SPIN

TRUTH 1: THE VALUE OF MARKETING IS DEFINED BY SALES

That's right. We're opening this book, written for marketers and chief-level executives, by telling you the cold truth about the business function of your livelihood. We posted the same statement on LinkedIn, and inspired a spirited discussion.

If you didn't get the chance to participate there, we'll give you the rest of this page to pause, consider it, and curse us out in writing in the blank space below.

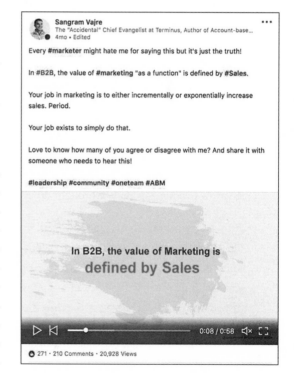

Sangram Vajre
The "Accidental" Chief Evangelist at Terminus, Author of Account-base...
4mo • Edited

Every #marketer might hate me for saying this but it's just the truth!

In #B2B, the value of #marketing "as a function" is defined by #Sales.

Your job in marketing is to either incrementally or exponentially increase sales. Period.

Your job exists to simply do that.

Love to know how many of you agree or disagree with me? And share it with someone who needs to hear this!

#leadership #community #oneteam #ABM

In B2B, the value of Marketing is
defined by Sales

0:08 / 0:58

271 · 210 Comments · 20,928 Views

_____
_____
_____
_____
_____
_____
_____
_____
_____
_____
_____

Many marketers might feel challenged or threatened by this notion. However, it isn't such a provocative idea. Remember, fewer than 1% of all leads turn into customers. That's hardly a statistic you want to stand behind. If company leaders set a 100% growth goal for a year, do they try to reach it by hiring more marketers? No! They might hire marketers to support sales, but there's no sales quota based on marketing.

It wasn't until we wrote our first book and piloted our first programs that we understood how much marketing is joined at the hip with sales.

It wasn't until we wrote our first book and piloted our first programs that we understood how much marketing is joined at the hip with sales. It's a rare company where the marketing department gets more money when sales go down. There's even a statistic that investors like to use as a growth metric when evaluating organizations: sales and marketing efficiency.

There are numerous examples of companies that have thrived for years without true marketing support, or even a marketing department. We've seen companies started by solo entrepreneurs file an initial public offering with a two-person marketing team. Sales will always be in the driver's seat, and marketers are brought on only to grow revenue—if they're brought on at all.

This might sound as if we're raining all over the marketing parade. But we find that aligning marketing with revenue frees designers and writers to do their best work, because they have a purpose to everything they create. You can design and write the heck out of ebooks, blog posts, and webinars, but if you don't know why you're making the effort, your creation may be vanishing into the void. These are what we call lost marketers, and the key to their salvation is a conversation about their role in creating demand to drive more business.

ABM *is* **B2B.**

Gifted with purpose, marketers are free to choose their tactics from a wider menu and communicate with a narrower audience. By running a well-thought-out B2B program, your marketing team structure will change. Your brand developers will become full-on field marketers and program managers, released from the monotony of siloed content. Suddenly, curated events, dinners, one-to-one videos, and more high-touch creative pieces are in play, because you identified them as marketing tactics that will generate revenue with select accounts.

Purpose-driven marketing doesn't go with the flow or stick to the same script for months. Instead, it builds excitement, aligns with your customers' goals, and brings marketing and sales together.

So don't be afraid or offended when we say that marketing is defined by sales. And don't look for so-called "ABM marketers" to replace your current team—there are no such creatures. Your current team will help send your revenue through the roof as long as you give them a greater and clearer purpose.

With the total number of leads as the ultimate measuring stick, the blame game starts as soon as sales numbers dip.

TRUTH 2: YOUR SILOS SHOULD BURN TO THE GROUND

Sales and marketing living together? Mass hysteria! Okay, we're paraphrasing Bill Murray's character in Ghostbusters, but these departments typically do not mix well. You might even say there has been an unhealthy rivalry between sales and marketing teams at most organizations. Both sides fight tirelessly for recognition as they work toward completely different goals: sales to drive revenue, and marketing to raise brand awareness or generate leads, no matter the quality. With the total number of leads as the ultimate measuring stick, the blame game starts as soon as sales numbers dip.

Do you recognize this rift at your company? Maybe you're reading this book because you know that something is broken, and you want to fix it.

At Terminus, we were raring to run with our first account-based program, and we made a list of 500 accounts to pursue. We couldn't wait to go to sales and say, "How do you like us now?!" But it didn't work that way. The sales representatives didn't care about our top 500 list. They didn't know the accounts, couldn't engage with them, and didn't make time for them. With 700-plus accounts already in each sales rep's portfolio, all we were doing was handing off a new heap of headaches.

So yeah, our first B2B program failed miserably. You can read all the gory details in the Maturity Curve section.

We quickly realized B2B is not a marketing thing that marketers should figure out. It's a business thing, and our job is to create business outcomes. Our program would never get off the ground if all we did was deliver hand-picked leads to sales; it would work only if we first asked sales what marketing could do to help them. Cats and dogs, under one roof.

The best organizations in the world act as #OneTeam. No matter how good your individual departments are, you can't operate together successfully if you have siloed goals.

One piece of common ground we found right away was the desire to make our jobs more efficient. What if we could reduce the number of accounts assigned to each sales rep to a maximum of 100? Then they could spend the time they previously wasted with dead ends getting to know everything about the best fits. A shared goal was born: Enable sales with metrics to engage only the accounts that could drive business outcomes.

Gone were the monthly state-of-the-union sales kickoffs in which marketers primed the goals deck for the sales leader. We were winning and losing together, which meant that we were meeting every day. We were strategizing every day, developing a shared language in real time, and giving ourselves a finite universe to work in. We were going all in, 100%, together.

#OneTeam: Sales team. Marketing team. Customer Success team.

Oh, you thought I forgot about CS? It's not surprising, considering that these unsung heroes of your organization lack the *rah-rah* enthusiasm of sales or the flashy events and websites of marketing. But you'll never find a great company with a lousy CS team, and vice versa. The number-one company killer isn't lack of growth; it's a poor retention rate.

What happens to all those customers after the hard work of a sales win? Your CS team members know, because they're the ones making your customers happy. Marketing and sales used to be responsible for figuring out where expansion opportunities were and which industries and companies were succeeding. You have a third department to fill in the knowledge gaps that inform your fit, intent, engagement models, and messaging strategy. Bring them in!

ABM isn't a marketing thing for marketers. It's a cross-functional approach to being account-centric and customer-obsessed. But it requires ownership and leadership from marketing to work as it's supposed to.

We can't stress enough: Bring them in, all of them, early and often. No one else could or should summon the troops, especially not your executives. It's up to the marketing leader to form this synergistic, multi-departmental beast. ABM isn't a marketing thing for marketers. It's a cross-functional approach to being account-centric and customer-obsessed. But it requires ownership and leadership from marketing to work as it's supposed to. Otherwise, it's like telling your teenage kids to behave and then leaving the room. Does that work for anyone, ever?

TRUTH 3: THE BUCK STOPS AT YOUR CEO

Marketers have over eleventy billion pieces of technology they can add to their stack. Maybe that number is closer to 8,000, but who's counting? Every evolution in B2B has been tech-driven, from email to marketing automation to predictive, and every new program has enticed marketers with the promise of making their job faster, better, and easier. Marketing's function has remained basically the same, while the tools have changed over time.

CEOs are driven by business outcomes and operational efficiency, so new tactics are judged against increasing leads, webinars, downloads, MQLs, and metrics that have been around for decades.

Does your marketing director tell your company CEO about every new piece of technology? Have you ever given a board member a heads-up on the hottest platform your department wanted to try? Did you ever need executive sign-off to buy a program that helps clone landing pages?

The answer is no. Because your CEO doesn't care. He or she generally is more focused on driving growth and ensuring the company has a brand they can be proud of.

One point of clarification: When we say CEO in this context, we don't necessarily mean the person who holds that job title. This person could be the head of a business unit in a large company or the actual CEO in a small but growing company. Our point is that this transformation will require buy-in from your C-level executives.

Tech-driven changes don't warrant a conversation with an executive because they don't affect organizational goals. **CEOs are driven by business outcomes and operational efficiency, so new tactics are judged against increasing leads, webinars, downloads, MQLs, and metrics that have been around for decades.** Your CEO or executive leader was trained by the company board, and the board was trained by the previous generation, that marketing's job is to build brand and create leads. ABM has been the first truly transformational strategy from a business perspective since the days of inbound. So the conversation must happen, and it must cover brand-new territory.

ABM *is* **B2B.**

You can't go rogue without executive support, because you'll be speaking two different languages when the time comes to gauge marketing success. Even if your transformed marketing program is knocking it out of the park to you, that won't mean anything to an executive who doesn't understand why the metrics are new and what it all means. And you might be out of a job.

Your CEOs know what ABM is. They know it works, and they know they should do it. But change is hard. CEOs and CMOs are still asking where the leads are, and it's your job to educate them why that's the wrong question. It's your job to show them why shrinking volume is a good thing when looking at accounts over leads. It's your job to sell them the idea of marketing and sales alignment. These are all big-time business transformations.

The good news is that you don't have to wait for executive sign-off to start a pilot B2B program. We learned early on the value of running short sprints to show success. Go to your executives with your universe already trimmed to the best-fit accounts, the right verticals, the ideal company sizes, and hammer home the concept of targeting and nurturing customers that will generate revenue (you know, speak the CEO language for a bit). Tell them you already have marketing, sales, and customer success teams aligned around the accounts you all agree are the most important. March in with a huge, 3D-printed funnel and dramatically flip it on the conference room table to make your point, if you have to. If your CEO finally says, "Great, go do B2B, but I still want to see 10,000 leads next month," at least you have a program that you can take to your next gig. In the Maturity Curve section, you will hear more examples of how companies of all sizes have done this successfully.

Again, executives aren't going to approach you and ask for a new way to do marketing. Once they understand and buy into concepts such as creating personal campaigns and seeking your ideal customers, they'll love B2B as much as you do. They just don't know it yet, so show them the money.

You need to stop measuring and reporting some vanity metrics and embrace the new ones focused on business outcomes.

TRUTH 4: YOUR VANITY IS MAKING YOUR MARKETING UGLY

Traditional marketing measurement is a lot like a fashion show. Model after model (or, in this case, metric after metric) saunter down the runway, each sporting splashier attire than the one before. They turn heads, they set off flashbulbs, and they promise to start trends. We're attracted to the spectacle, but what does it all get you in the end? You're not going to wear any of these outfits, anyway.

You need to stop measuring and reporting some vanity metrics, and embrace the new ones focused on business outcomes. Here's an example:

WHAT TO STOP AND START MEASURING

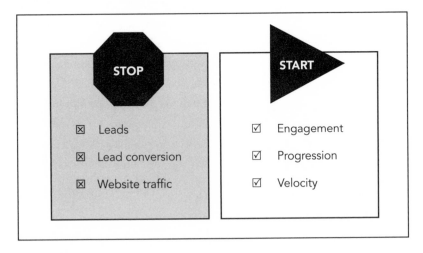

STOP

☒ Leads
☒ Lead conversion
☒ Website traffic

START

☑ Engagement
☑ Progression
☑ Velocity

Here's what TOPO said in its 2019 account-based benchmark research report: "Account-based strategies deliver business outcomes, not vanity metrics. Account-based is not a campaign or technology purchase. It is a strategic go-to-market decision delivering key board-level metrics. Respondents indicate that account-based improves customer lifetime value (80%), improves win rates (86%), and delivers higher ROI (76%) than a traditional go-to-market approach."

The marketing you're used to is obsessed with vanity metrics. It makes sense—total number of leads is a sexy number when you're killing the inbound game. And you know what's sexier than a whole bunch of leads? A whole bunch more leads. That's the narcissistic world marketers lived in pre-ABM, and it's taken years of practicing and refining our strategies to understand what real measurement beauty looks like.

For years, marketers were lured by the siren song of demand generation, only to crash on the rocks when it came to converting a sale. The same is true with website traffic. If you create five press releases a year, you might have five spikes a year—but is it the best traffic? Marketers weren't asking themselves the right questions, and they certainly weren't digging deeper into the funnel to pull out better metrics.

That all changed for us when we saw how organizational shifts to B2B affected not only acquisition, but also pipeline velocity, engagement, and retention. Suddenly, we had brand-new metrics that told a more complete story, even if our vanity numbers dropped. When we started focusing on business outcomes, we could look back and see how our pretty numbers were clouding our opportunities for success. We didn't just look at how many people downloaded an ebook or registered for a webinar; we asked ourselves how many of those people were part of our total addressable market. We found that although this number was a smaller percentage, we were moving deals much more quickly, and engaging with a select few accounts much more deeply.

ABM = B2B is a mindset shift.

As we've said before, ABM = B2B is a mindset shift. For years, marketers and executives have been trained that charts going up and to the right are good. You'll read later about one customer who started a B2B program and immediately saw website traffic drop 30%. Their first reaction was, "Oh s***, we messed up!" Upon closer inspection, 70% of their traffic was coming from non-target accounts. What a waste of time to care about all those dead ends! So the customer stopped prioritizing false metrics of success and embraced the idea of down and to the right being good for business.

To start doing something better, you must stop doing something else. That might seem vague, but B2B is really about taking the most efficient route to reach the right customers. Vanity metrics make your job harder. We saw another customer cut their marketing tech stack from 22 technologies to six after starting the new program and still grow revenue. What marketer wouldn't love that?

We will give you the proper metrics throughout the new funnel, which we call the One Scorecard, later in this book so you'll know what to measure and report. We can't promise that it will be as sexy as what you're used to, but we can promise that the revenue coming your way will be a real thing of beauty.

TRUTH 5: STRATEGY EATS YOUR TACTICS FOR BREAKFAST

Like mad scientists in a lab, we were unaware of what we unleashed when we started running our first B2B programs. We knew we had created an acquisition monster, and we were more than satisfied to flip the funnel and change demand gen for the better.

What we were doing felt fresh—finding the best-fit accounts, finding the right people to engage with, and turning them into advocates. And it was fresh. We were passing accounts to sales that we knew would drive business... but that's as far as we went.

From our perspective as marketers, we added all the value we could during the acquisition phase. It was almost unheard of then for marketing to have input further along the pipeline, let alone with customer marketing. Our supposed account-based strategy was essentially a targeting tactic—an effective one, but a tactic nonetheless.

> **It was almost unheard of then for marketing to have input further along the pipeline, let alone with customer marketing.**

Then something funny happened. Our customers who saw the benefits of the way we were doing things for acquisition started applying the same thinking to the rest of the pipeline. We saw companies running revenue-producing velocity campaigns we'd never thought of before. One of our biggest early stories of customer success was an IT company that applied account-based thinking to cross-sell, up-sell (or up-serve, as we like to call it), and mentor current customers. We had never considered that. Suddenly, ABM was proving to be a multifaceted strategy adaptable for the entire customer life cycle.

It hit us like a ton of bricks. Of course, it's great to focus on accounts that have already raised their hands, and engage other people within those accounts to increase velocity. Of course, it makes sense to cross-sell and up-serve current customers whose pain points you already know, under the engagement terms you're already using. It was exciting for us to see others being so creative with our marketing baby. Now we felt like mad scientists, and every time we witnessed a new take on ABM, we screamed, "It's alive!"

> **Doing B2B at its finest doesn't mean you can have one tool that does everything.**

Now we're at a fork in the road for businesses: Either rethink your revenue strategy, or keep trucking with traditional demand generation. You must decide what is right for your business. Doing B2B at its finest doesn't mean you can have one tool that does everything. The pieces must come together,

There's pressure to see immediate growth with account-centric programs to validate the decision to transform.

so now you should start thinking of all the plays you can run to engage in a meaningful way. This involves connecting direct mail, advertising, landing pages, webinars—all tactics you already use. How they all fit together now is the strategy, the monster you develop that can't wait to escape the lab to do amazing things for your whole pipeline and business.

That's at the heart and mind of this book. If you're a B2B marketer, and you don't know who you're selling to, what are you doing? If the answer is anything except strategizing, you'll get eaten alive.

TRUTH 6: YOU CAN'T BENCH-PRESS 500 POUNDS ON DAY ONE

If you're a marketer who happens to be a world-class power lifter, we apologize for underestimating your strength. For mere mortals, racking weight after weight and expecting to crush eight to 10 repetitions without a foundation of fitness would be foolish at best and dangerous at worst. However, you'd never walk away from the bench feeling like a failure and deciding never to jog, ride a bike, or do push-ups or crunches again just because you couldn't lift two or three times your body weight. If you were serious about bench-pressing 500 pounds, you'd find your baseline weight and try to beat it a little at a time, day by day. Just don't skip leg day, or so we've heard.

When we first tried to transform our growing business with an account-centric program, we were the scrawny gym rat confidently gripping the bar with no spotter in sight. Our 500 pounds took the form of 500 accounts, and we didn't raise it even an inch off the rack. We were trying to change too much, too soon, and expecting all the results to fall into place exactly as we envisioned them. We wanted instant gratification in an incremental world.

For established companies deeply rooted in marketing processes that are fairly successful, the idea of starting fresh with a new routine can seem daunting. There's pressure to see immediate growth with account-centric programs to validate the decision to transform. The bottom line is that until you run several of these programs across acquisition, acceleration, and expansion, you don't see everything that surrounds it as a strategy. It takes time, scale, and reps to figure things out.

After our bench-pressing failure, we moved to the cardio area of the marketing gym and started running sprints. That was when data became our best friend. We ran a campaign for 10 accounts instead of 500, and saw engagement in five of them. Great! We got sales involved with those five, brushed the rest to the side, and swapped in five new accounts. The standard marketing strategy would be to run a nurture program for all of them, no matter what the data said. But account-centric programs allow you to stop, see what's going on, reflect, change, and adapt. Think of it as interval training.

The other critical piece we learned, which is where so many organizations fail today, is that a killer strategy doesn't guarantee results even on a small scale. There's no timetable for everything to click into place. You can look in the mirror after one day at the gym and not see anything different. Day two, same thing. But what will you look like a year from now? You must commit to finding out.

Your first pilot might be one campaign for one customer. That's not a failure, but an incredible opportunity to define your metrics of success. Patterns start to develop, and you can double down on what works and take away what doesn't as you slowly increase the intensity. When you get in the weeds, you learn about customer engagement styles. Not everyone will engage on direct mail, landing pages, or video, so maybe you don't need to do every option when just one will do the trick.

But for the love of kettlebells, keep iterating! The biggest barrier we see to implementing an account-based program is a bias toward inaction. Falling back into old habits, no matter how fruitful they are, is putting you further behind. When you're training with the same weight you always have, how can you expect to stimulate new muscle growth?

Whether it's strategizing about the best way to reach a select group of accounts, demonstrating your value to sales throughout the life cycle, or even selling an organizational switch to your executive team, never try to show off your strength if you don't have it yet. Every organization has the frame to support massive gains, and as your personal marketing trainers, we're here to make sure you fill it out in the healthiest way possible.

TRUTH 7: SOME ACCOUNTS DESERVE CHAMPAGNE; OTHERS SPARKLING WATER.

Make a list of all the marketing activities you do today. How many things are on it? Forty? Fifty?

So many you've lost count? Now think of the thousands of companies you're going after, or the hundreds you've identified as the best fits. It's impossible to do all things for all current or future customers, even though you'd like to.

Not all accounts are equal in value, so why are you creating equal experiences for them?

Not all accounts are equal in value, so why are you creating equal experiences for them? It's okay to play favorites—in fact, it's necessary! Assigning tiers is the fairest way to make sure you design experiences that reflect what each account is worth. Your top tier gets wined and dined; your bottom tier gets Sprite and takeout. A B2B approach gives such powerful insights into your accounts that you can decide how much to care about each of them.

If you have an account that's worth a million dollars, care more! Pour everything you have into focused direct mail, a landing page with content tailored to that account and your support, a microsite all about them, a private dinner, and anything else that acknowledges how valuable the account is to you.

It's okay to play favorites—in fact, it's necessary!

At the same time, a thousand-dollar account might not get a specific landing page, but you might take them to a page showing that you understand the

ABM *is* **B2B.**

industry and have supported other companies within it. Trust us, even though your lower-tier accounts aren't getting the steak house treatment, B2B lends itself to impressive personalization, especially in contrast to the traditional approach most companies experience.

With your high-value clients, if you care the most, you're going to win the most. We'll take a red-eye flight from Los Angeles to London for a one-hour dinner if a million-dollar check is on the line. We've done enough dinners in recent years to understand the value of being a facilitator. We don't organize dinners to pitch potential customers one-on-one; that's a sales trick, and they see right through it. Instead, we invite CMOs from their industry who happen to be our customers and position the dinner as a networking event, an opportunity to meet people they otherwise wouldn't. While they're in the same room, the conversation inevitably will drift to your product and platform. Voila! You've created a memorable experience that shows how much you care and the value you bring.

Dinners are just one way to make meaningful connections. If a $10,000 check is on the line, we'll hop on Zoom and demonstrate value in other ways. Experiences vary depending on your target. If it's a high-tech customer, advertising may work best. Doctors and nurses respond better to direct mail. IT pros spend a lot of time on forums. At Terminus, we sell to marketing and sales people who spend more time on LinkedIn, so that's where we post. We're not on Snapchat, thank goodness. Account-based programs show where your people are, so meet them there, and tier your engagements appropriately. Follow the money, as they say.

Care the most, win the most. It's why we do a daily podcast to offer a free LinkedIn Learning Account-Based Marketing Foundations course, and that's why we published the second book on this topic when few others in our industry had written one. We don't have to do any of it, but we care so much about B2B marketing that we must share our excitement and our findings. We want to give voice to people who are doing incredible things and show how others have helped us succeed.

So there you have it: seven lessons we didn't know when we put pen to paper four years ago. When people learn later, a lot of them say, "If I only knew then what I know now." We don't feel that way. We're happy we didn't have all the answers from the beginning. The failures, false starts, and tough times made us stronger and better, and our customer successes, many achieved despite our shortcomings, propelled us to greater heights.

The rest of this book is filled with practical guidance for taking your B2B marketing from average to good to great with an account-centric mindset. You'll read stories of customers who solved specific problems like yours by applying all sorts of programs. No matter what size, industry, or program you're running, if you're in B2B, we have an example for you of how another company has completely transformed its organization to grow efficiently at scale.

Now you know what we've learned.

It's time to do some teaching.

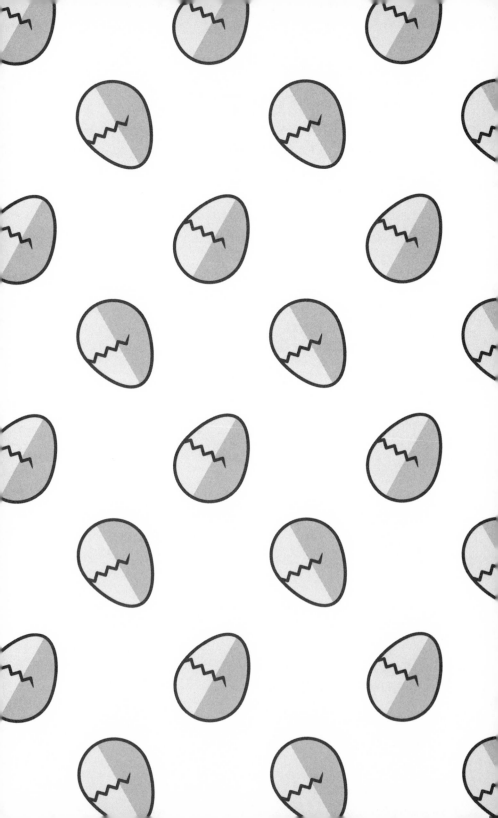

SECTION 2:

THE MATURITY CURVE

Going from Status Quo to B2B 2.0

Sometimes you just don't know what you don't know. That's where we were four years ago, when we wrote the first book on account-based marketing. Did we let the blind spots in our knowledge stop us from writing that book and kick-starting a business revolution? Of course not. Everything we said, taught, and acted on when we started running ABM programs was spot on for the marketing mindset at the time.

Hop into a time machine back to the middle of this decade, and survey the B2B landscape. Suddenly, you're in a world where leads are king, demand generation gurus are winning awards, and automation specialists are hailed as heroes. It's a world built on form fills, MQLs, sales readiness, and sales handoffs, but one that lacks meaningful insight into who's entering the pipeline.

Few companies were practicing ABM at that time, even in small sprints. When we wrote the first book on the method, we knew we had found a better way, but we didn't know what it would look like in practice over time. We didn't have enough data to reach any conclusions.

In recent years, as ABM has gone from a marketing trend to a business transformation, we've been able to study the shift. In fact, FlipMyFunnel conducted a comprehensive survey of ABM practitioners at the end of 2018, using three years of data to learn how companies are utilizing ABM and how much success they're achieving. We definitely uncovered some trends worth noting.

There are a ton of great insights in the full report on FlipMyFunnel.com (and it's free!), but here's the bottom line:

We found that the majority of companies who have committed to ABM are still in the early stages of implementation.

ABM IMPLEMENTATION ACROSS ORGANIZATIONS (2018)

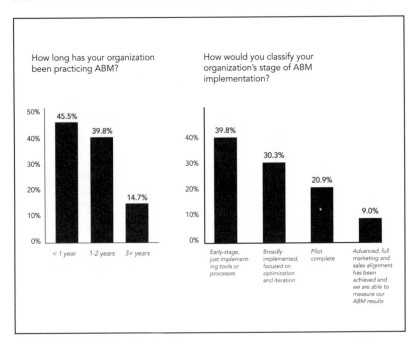

What this tells us is that many companies are figuring out the growing pains between marketing worlds. They have a toe dipped in the water of 1:1 engagement, but their other foot is planted in the land of artificially qualifying leads. Some companies are stretched out, with one hand in a targeting pilot program, and the other relying on reactive sales tactics. Basically, companies are playing ABM Maturity Twister. And that's totally fine!

Techniques seen as the status quo of marketing today, such as lead generation and MQLs, were marketing nirvana from 2005 to 2015. You were a rock star on the stage when you showed MQLs and funnel conversion rates and won awards for your work.

No one ever said a paradigm shift wasn't without its awkward transitions. We would even venture out to say that as email is the fuel for Marketing Automation, targeted advertising is the fuel for ABM. And now, with new data, surveys, and customer stories we've witnessed, we can see what's possible when we look at ABM as B2B. In turn, companies that are finding their way and jumping in with their own programs finally can plot where they are on their ABM journey.

We call it the B2B Maturity Curve.

B2B MATURITY CURVE

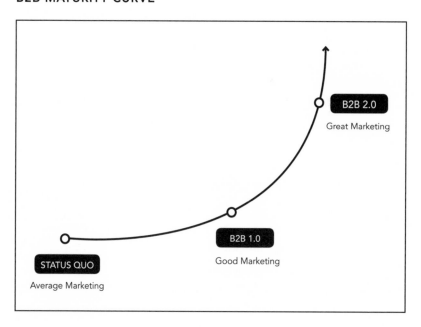

The curve is simple, yet dynamic. Ask any company if they would prefer to be average or great with their marketing, and you know what they'd say. But they're not all where they want to be yet. Within this curve is a roadmap outlining the movement from status quo to B2B 2.0 across every key component of ABM marketing, sales, and customer success, making it abundantly clear that most organizations haven't reached full maturity.

As you saw in our survey, only 9% of companies self-identify as mature enough to drive their B2B to greatness.

What does that say about the other 91%? Are they failures? Of course not!

It also should be pointed out that companies who've achieved B2B 2.0 haven't won, either. There are always ways to improve. Most companies struggle with ABM at the beginning, simply because they don't know where they fall on the stages of the B2B Maturity Curve, so they don't know what to do first.

They just don't know what they don't know.

Not anymore.

This chart gives you insight into various components of the B2B curve, and you should be able to recognize where you align based on the programs you've tried or managed to run. If you put a checkmark where you self-identify in each row, you'll form your own unique pattern. Just because you're status quo in one aspect doesn't prevent you from being firmly in B2B 1.0 or B2B 2.0 in another. That's part of playing the game of B2B Maturity Twister.

Here are a few things to note as you read this chart:

An average or a status quo program might help you grow in the short term, but not over the long term, and it won't be uber-efficient. As you progress into a good program, you should see that efficient growth is possible, but not yet at scale while you focus on a few segments. Only when you begin your march toward "greatness" will you start to see efficient growth at scale.

This is the B2B nirvana, where we hope you'll find yourself after reading this book.

B2B MATURITY FRAMEWORK

Status Quo (where you've been)	B2B 1.0 (where you might be)	B2B 2.0 (where you are going)
Disconnected: Leads at all cost	**Static:** Pilot program "Top 100 list"	**Dynamic:** Run you biz at scale "Always on"
Quantity	**Quality**	**Experiential**
Reactive sales alerts	**Proactive** sales alerts	**Prioritized** sales alerts
Funnel	Double Funnel	One Scorecard
CRM + MA	7000+ shiny new objects — best of breed	TEAM-based tech stack — smaller and tightly integrated
Sales-driven or Marketing-driven	Marketing + Sales Alignment	Sales + Marketing + CS acting as #OneTeam
Inefficient growth	Efficient **growth** model **in isolation**	**Efficient growth model at scale**

Your eventual goal is to reach efficient growth at scale, but you can't get there overnight. The maturity curve gives you a game plan to say, "OK, in the next 30 to 60 to 90 days, I'm going to move from a leads-at-all-cost approach to targeting my top 100 accounts using a pilot program. Or, "I'm going to stop measuring two funnels and commit to one B2B scorecard."

Dedication, patience and time are the only things that separate a successful B2B program from the rest. Your capacity to thoughtfully measure and analyze your outputs while trial'ing and error'ing around your inputs will give you a big advantage over organizations looking for a quick fix. It takes patience to see the gaps in your program, time to make adjustments and dedication to trust your strategic lens that ties it all together.

Where do you stand on the B2B Maturity Curve? Before you make that assessment, look at the examples set by a few of our favorite success stories.

All of these companies we've worked with started by understanding where their current marketing efforts stood. The five stories show how transformative ABM is for entire organizations as they moved from status quo to a completely new form of marketing.

These aren't merely good stories. They're Good to Great ones.

You can read them all or quickly see, based on the strategy and size, which company aligns most closely with your business model.

Company	Industry	Problem	Strategy	Solution
Thomson Reuters	Mass Media	Lack of resources to personalize for high-value accounts	Acquisition, Acceleration, Expansion	A combination of high-touch and high-tech programs
Results: 95% win-rate with deals within the ABM program.				
Masergy	Telecom	Inefficient customer acquisition strategy	Acquisition, Expansion	Multi-channel engagement strategy
Results: Avg. sales cycle length was reduced by 10%, 50% increase in deal size, A 250% increase in account penetration.				
Pramata	Revenue Software	Too many tools	Acquisition	Consolidated tech stack
Results: 60% reduction in cost of acquisition of customers, 2.5x increase in mid-funnel pipeline.				
Snowflake	Data Software	Lack of refinement and alignment	Acquisition, Acceleration	1:1 campaigns at scale
Results: Over 50% of monthly content downloads on Snowflake's site were driven by dedicated, collaborative 1:1 ABM campaigns.				

Company	Industry	Problem	Strategy	Solution
Sigstr	Martech	Too many manual processes	Acquisition	Scaling from 1 company targeting to 1000

Results: Ability to do personalized campaign across 2,000 accounts with repeatable process.

Company	Industry	Problem	Strategy	Solution
Terminus	Martech	Too many spreadsheets	Acquisition, Acceleration	A single scorecard

Results: Opportunity conversion rate increased by 78%, Sales cycle decrease by 20 days.

THOMSON REUTERS - WHEN A 95% WIN RATE BECOMES THE NORM

Thomson Reuters is the world's leading provider of news and information-based tools to professionals. Our worldwide network of journalists and specialist editors keep customers up to speed on global developments, with a particular focus on legal, regulatory, and tax changes. Thomson Reuters shares are listed on the Toronto and New York Stock Exchanges. For more information on Thomson Reuters, visit tr.com, and for the latest world news, reuters.com

WHERE THEY WERE (STATUS QUO)

The size of a corporation doesn't always equal the scale of its ABM program. For media giant Thomson Reuters, home to nearly 30,000 employees worldwide and more than $11 billion in annual revenue, the challenge was to retain its highest-risk customers, the ones it absolutely could not afford to lose, in the major-revenue-driving legal division.

The early forays into ABM were small steps up from a traditional, reactive, email-based marketing strategy. The company had buy-in and alignment across sales and marketing, plus a large opportunity to operate at scale to close more deals.

What Thomson Reuters really wanted to do was blow out its digital ABM efforts. That was easier said than done. Email marketing had great reach, but low impact. The small ABM team at Thomson Reuters didn't have the resources to give its highest-value customers the personalized experiences that would generate results.

The question became how to focus on the right number of accounts to enable sales with the tools and data to build lifelong relationships with customers, at scale, while keeping an eye on win rate at the metric that mattered most.

WHERE THEY WENT (B2B 1.0)

Thomson Reuters built a dedicated ABM team that was four people strong: a department head, a marketing specialist, and two ABM managers. What that team lacked in size it more than made up for in strategic brilliance, especially when it came to organizational alignment. Because this ABM effort was so focused on retaining current customers, Thomson Reuters knew it wasn't enough to be aligned just between sales and marketing; sales and account management had to be working as one team, too. No one knows an account better than the people working on it every day, and this partnership established trust that sales would be enabled with the correct strategy for key accounts.

> Thomson Reuters knew it wasn't enough to be aligned just between sales and marketing; sales and account management had to be working as one team, too.

With full organizational buy-in established, Thomson Reuters committed to focusing its account-centric efforts on 250 accounts. The list comprised can't-lose accounts up for renewal within 12 to 18 months as well as the largest accounts deemed best-fit to acquire.

Once Thomson Reuters turned its account-centric program on, it never shut it off. Tactically, the ABM team leveraged new digital efforts such as personalized web experiences, gamification, more robust email and web marketing, and routine surveys to stay on top of customer needs.

Building an always-on ABM program also meant that Thomson Reuters had to review its list constantly to make sure it was hitting the most important accounts. The sole focus was on creating valuable, positive experiences with current and future customers with every touchpoint, so the team coordinated with sales and account managers to move priorities around when necessary. Customers in the early stages of a long renewal cycle were put on hold with a marketing strategy, then re-engaged with sales at a more tactical level when the time was right.

Focusing on just a few accounts and scaling wide allowed Thomson Reuters to deploy an unceasing program that wouldn't have been possible in a traditional marketing approach. Including all accounts in an account-centric program was impossible, so it became critical to evaluate the most important techniques and tactics that would achieve scale within their target list and resources.

Thomson Reuters landed on a combination of high-touch and high-tech to create powerful, blended messaging strategies. The marketing team created personalized web experiences based on IP backtracking data and leveraged online content syndication while sending impactful direct mail and attending relevant events. This approach allowed the team to identify what worked efficiently, and to modify messages quickly to replicate that success with other accounts.

WHERE THEY ARE (B2B 2.0)

Thomson Reuters successfully identified accounts the company couldn't afford to lose and others it really wanted to win, then threw the ABM kitchen

Thomson Reuters measured a 95% win rate from deals in its ABM program.

sink at them to grow meaningful relationships. The result was a successful program that would be simply unbelievable if it weren't actually true. Here's its own paragraph to drive the point home:

Results: Thomson Reuters measured a 95% win rate from deals in its ABM program. Wowzers.

As part of the measurement, Thomson Reuters set a goal of 75% of ABM accounts having at least two digital touchpoints included in their account plan and acted on, a goal they exceeded in year one. The initial success of the program allowed Thomson Reuters to scale up to more than 500 accounts, providing the same personalized level driven by digital efforts.

All successful ABM programs feature quarterly, monthly, or even weekly account reviews to keep everyone on the same page and looking at what's working and what can be improved upon as #OneTeam. Thomson Reuters takes it even further by treating the sales and account management teams as though they are customers. The ABM team sends out twice-yearly surveys to check the program's pulse, asking sales and account managers where they're seeing value and giving them a platform to provide feedback. This helps the organization make future investments in the right places.

Thomson Reuters shows the power of ABM in generating big results for big companies, even with a small, dedicated team in charge. With marketers focusing on revenue and sales enabled to get personal at scale, maybe winning at a staggeringly high level isn't so surprising after all.

ABM *is* **B2B.**

MASERGY: THE UPSIDE TO UP-SERVING (NOT UPSELLING) WITH ABM

Masergy enables global enterprises to innovate, disrupt, and dominate their industries with transformative solutions in managed SD-WAN, cloud communications, and managed security. Built on the world's most innovative Software Defined Platform, our agile technologies, customizable solutions, and unmatched customer experience are why leading organizations rely on Masergy to stay ahead of the competition. Learn more at masergy.com

WHERE THEY WERE (STATUS QUO)

What would you do if you acquired 25,000 new leads in a year and a half? Shout it from the rooftops? Throw a party? Invent elaborate high fives? Masergy did all that and more to celebrate its incredible demand gen success. But the good times came to a screeching halt once those leads failed to turn into sales. As quickly as they entered the pipeline, these dead-end leads were swept up and thrown into the trash with the rest of the deflated party balloons.

It was an understatement to say that Masergy had an inefficient customer acquisition strategy. The firm wanted to go big, because that's how business gets done for Texas-based organizations, especially this software solutions company for enterprise networks, cybersecurity, and cloud communications. Name a global giant, and chances are, it's a competitor. Masergy had seen success through its channel-focused marketing tactics, but if its leaders wanted to win at the worldwide level, they had to bring in new revenue streams from even more channels.

So they committed to lead-gen volume and chipped in big time. Inbound marketing tactics expanded to include AdWords campaigns, pay-per-click, and content syndication. Company staffers made sure to attend as many events as possible based on where they thought their customers would be. They spent a lot of money, and they saw leads roll in by the tens of thousands.

> **The volume was so high, and the insights were so lackluster, that sales were stuck in the mud with more dirt piling on daily.**

As Masergy quickly discovered, this disconnected acquisition strategy was a nightmare for the sales team. Sales knew the leads were bad—the number of uninterested prospects, or what we like to call future customers, made that clear—but they didn't know which ones were bad. Even worse, they didn't know which ones were good. The volume was so high, and the insights were so lackluster that sales were stuck in the mud with more dirt piling on daily.

WHERE THEY WENT (B2B 1.0)

The folks at Masergy needed to define a few things. First, which companies were most likely to buy from them? They offer a unique solution that isn't one-size-fits-all, and their traditional approach to lead generation failed to match the complexity of customer needs. To drive demand from the right types of new accounts, Masergy analyzed what their best customers looked like and built an Ideal Customer Profile based on specific criteria.

In addition to driving more sales-qualified accounts, Masergy expected to see an increase in the number of connections with individual decision-makers or influencers from target accounts. This enhanced account penetration could occur only by focusing marketing and sales outreach on a select few accounts.

Instead of 25,000 traditional leads delivering a scattershot range of potential customers, being able to hand over best-fit accounts to sales reps transformed Masergy's approach from batch-and-blast to well-crafted, 1:1 engagement.

Masergy completely overhauled their organizational set-up around ABM. Their sales reps began to focus on 20 high-value accounts during 6 to 12 months, and their business development reps managed a list of 50 accounts. This setup let them focus on creating personalized experiences backed up by intent data. They knew who their customers were and what triggered the unique form of outreach that advanced them along the pipeline.

One of Masergy's target accounts was a major airline. Their multi-channel engagement strategy for this account included 1:1 ads, outbound calls with personalized messaging and direct mail, and email nurture programs that kept their brand in front of all the key stakeholders at the airline.

To activate their sales team based on website visits, Masergy routed accounts to three internal teams: BDR, channel, and outside sales.

For example, a high-performing early ad triggered a BDR to reach out with a free ebook about their solution or a case study specific to their industry. That was great timing for both the future customer and the BDR.

Results: Masergy's average sales cycle length was reduced by 10%, roughly equivalent to one month. They also noticed a 50% increase in deal size, 50% more opportunity conversion with their best-fit accounts, and a 250% increase in account penetration.

> Their multi-channel engagement strategy for this account included 1:1 ads, outbound calls with personalized messaging and direct mail, and email nurture programs that kept their brand in front of all the key stakeholders at the airline

WHERE THEY ARE (B2B 2.0)

Acquisition and pipeline velocity were just the tips of the iceberg when it came to Masergy's good-to-great transformation. What they did next blew our minds, and showed us an ABM possibility we hadn't even considered: growing accounts beyond the initial sales win.

Masergy's flagship product drives 75% of its revenue, so many customers weren't aware of the full extent of their other, complementary solutions.

Masergy's account managers always lead with the hero product during the sales cycle, but the focus shifts to cross-selling security and voice solutions after the sale.

The Masergy story of good to great is B2B at its most dynamic. It showed us the power of an always-on approach to marketing and the way this strategy applied to every aspect of a customer relationship. It was no surprise that Masergy was awarded the 2018 SiriusDecisions ABM Program of the Year Award.

We watched in real time as Masergy teams applied the same strategies from the acquisition phase toward customer retention. They gathered data and learned about customer challenges to identify opportunities to cross-sell. Marketers and account managers aligned on 1:1 engagement campaigns tailored to specific customer cases. They were ready with the perfect message at the perfect time, just as if they were trying to acquire a new customer. It was genius. By applying this approach to their current customer base, Masergy saw five times as much engagement from targeted accounts and a 40% increase in opportunity creation. And because they kept personal relationships and continued to serve relevant, high-touch content, their net promoter score jumped from 70% to 90%. Customers were delighted, and so were we at watching a customer do so much with an account-based strategy.

The Masergy story of good to great is B2B at its most dynamic. It showed us the power of an always-on approach to marketing, and the way this strategy applied to every aspect of a customer relationship. It was no surprise that Masergy was awarded the 2018 SiriusDecisions ABM Program of the Year Award.

PRAMATA - DRIVING BETTER RESULTS WITH LESS TRAFFIC AND FEWER TOOLS

Pramata helps large B2B enterprises eliminate revenue leakage. Pramata has created millions of dollars in value for some of the largest companies in the world, including Allergan, CenturyLink, Comcast Business, Cyxtera, FICO, NCR, Micro Focus, Novelis, Rackspace, and Vertafore. Headquartered in Brisbane, CA, Pramata also has offices in Kansas City, MO, and Bangalore, India. Learn more at pramata.com.

WHERE THEY WERE (STATUS QUO)

Have you ever tried to sell a solution to a problem that most people don't even know exists? That's Pramata's challenge. The Bay Area-based company uses human-in-the-loop AI technology to help large B2B companies eliminate revenue leakage, which is a nasty-sounding term for losses due to inefficiencies and mismanagement.

The types of companies Pramata works with are prone to these errors. The organizations typically have $300 million-plus in revenue with long sales cycles, lots of products and services, and extremely complex customer relationships, some still on paper. This complexity means that billing mistakes are common, churn is inevitable, and upselling and renegotiating are almost impossible.

At a company of 10,000 employees, maybe 20 people know about revenue leakage. They are typically high-level operational leaders and financial executives, hardly the easiest people to connect with, and certainly not the audience one would expect to fill out a form on Pramata's website. Many large B2B organizations have invested unsuccessfully in fixing their revenue leakage and come to the skeptical conclusion that it's just the cost of doing business.

Pramata insiders had a lot of persuading to do, and their marketing was broad in scope compared with the number of people who cared. They were

This led to 70% of Pramata's website traffic coming from non-target accounts.

focusing on content syndication to get website form fills, which was working from a vanity metric perspective. But the data told the real story: The people who filled out the forms came from lower-level leadership positions, and didn't know or care about the problem. This led to 70% of Pramata's website traffic coming from non-target accounts.

This one-size-fits-all strategy was not generating the number of opportunities the company wanted. Sales cycles were longer than needed because the wrong people were at the table, and deals stalled before an ideal executive-level customer ever became aware of Pramata. To bust out of status quo, Pramata needed to shake things up by shrinking the system down.

WHERE THEY WENT (B2B 1.0)

Pramata went right to the top with its initial ABM program, targeting sales ops and finance executives at 332 tech companies. They rebuilt the entire process and optimized tactics with the goal of simplifying everything. The first move? Eliminating the pointless form fills on their website. CFOs weren't searching for Pramata, and engagements with people who were visiting the site were meaningless.

Pramata quickly understood that education had to come before engagement. Their small sales and marketing teams worked together to develop personalized messaging aimed at the few individuals who understood the problem of revenue leakage. Paring down the target list allowed Pramata's sales team to research the 10 to 20 people who cared and drive them to the website or curated event.

When they dug back into the data, Pramata staffers saw something that would cause most organizations to push the panic button: Website traffic had dropped nearly 10% in one quarter. But they knew better than to take a vanity metric at face value. What actually happened was that 70% of all traffic now came from the top 332 accounts, exactly the ones Pramata wanted on the site. Although the total of people was smaller, the number the company could sell to was far larger.

Pramata didn't need thousands of leads per quarter because its deal sizes were large, and high customer satisfaction meant almost a 100% retention rate. Teams knew if they could attract better leads, they could close more deals and butter their bread with upselling. Among their customers, 75% grew five to ten times within two years of the initial deal.

Through an account-centric approach focused on targeting the right people and spreading the knowledge about revenue leakage, Pramata increased its inbound lead volume from one per quarter to five to seven, halving their deal time with those leads.

> **Pramata didn't need thousands of leads per quarter because its deal sizes were large, and high customer satisfaction meant almost a 100% retention rate.**

WHERE THEY ARE (B2B 2.0)

Pramata embraced its shrinking numbers as it started over. Instead trying to force the square peg of inefficient processes and tools into the round hole of a B2B model, the organization made sure its process fully supported its strategy. The target list was trimmed and more manageable, the website traffic went down and led to more deals, and the tech stack shrank from 22 tools to six. A more efficient tool set allowed Pramata to decrease costs and still deliver on strategy.

Results: Pramata's experiential program has delivered results that actually matter for the audiences they're targeting and customers they're nurturing.

A few greatest hits include:

- 60% reduction in the cost of customer acquisition compared with demand generation

- 4-times increase in sales-accepted leads

- 81% decrease in the cost of a sales-accepted lead

- 32% reduction in average deal time

- 2.5-times increase in mid-funnel pipeline

Companies faced with complex problems often throw more complicated solutions on the fire. The good-to-great story of Pramata shows the power of dialing it down, getting smarter, and doing much more with way less.

SNOWFLAKE - THE FUTURE BELONGS TO THE ONES WHO CAN FORECAST

Snowflake is the only data warehouse built for the cloud, enabling the data-driven enterprise with instant elasticity, secure data sharing, and per-second pricing across multiple clouds. Snowflake combines the power of data warehousing, the flexibility of big data platforms, and the elasticity of the cloud at a fraction of the cost of traditional solutions. Snowflake: Your data, no limits. Find out more at snowflake.com.

WHERE THEY WERE (STATUS QUO)

With a company name like Snowflake, creating unique customer experiences must be the heart of the business. That's why Snowflake, a cloud-based data management solution, was willing to take a big risk and adopt an ABM program more than two years ago.

We say big risk because ABM was a buzzword at that time. Not many marketers were willing to stake their careers on being ABM practitioners. Snowflake started with just one ABM employee, who was engaged in an unspoken rivalry with his demand-gen counterpart. Who grew the business more? Whose philosophy reigned supreme?

Snowflake started running account-based plays with the goal of getting high-priority accounts to click on their display ads. They were content-creation machines, and extremely aggressive in their approach. They tried everything, including the use of customer names and logos on ads, which resulted in a few cease-and-desist legal letters. Their hunger to drive business outcomes through ABM was apparent, but they lacked refinement and alignment.

WHERE THEY WENT (B2B 1.0)

As they began to iterate and learn from their first programs, Snowflake staffers saw the value of being prescriptive instead of focusing on clickbait tactics. They got smarter at creating content experiences that added value to their customers' days.

Snowflake grew to a team of six dedicated ABM marketers in addition to their Inbound marketing team, assigned to different regions across the country. Each team became responsible for running 200 concurrent 1:1 campaigns built on bespoke content experiences and personalized messaging. They created tailored landing pages for each account, empowering sales to choose content based on insights driven by marketing.

> Each team became responsible for running 200 concurrent 1:1 campaigns built on bespoke content experiences and personalized messaging.

Snowflake has always been driven by its philosophy that marketing sets the boundaries. Yes, ABM is a function of driving sales outcomes, but salespeople are hired and given accounts to cover because of the data uncovered through ABM. That's why the ABM team at Snowflake emphasized supporting sales at every touchpoint, from enabling sales with account intelligence for better discovery-call experiences to creating landing pages, ad groups, and segments in their ABM platform.

Ads evolved from "Snowflake + your company name" to "Hey, customer, here's how we can help you solve one specific problem." As the team members put it, they wanted viewers to understand they'd just been "ABM'ed."

After previous messaging efforts sometimes got them in hot water, Snowflake refined its approach to make ad viewers aware that a content experience was just around the corner. Ads evolved from "Snowflake + your company name" to "Hey, customer, here's how we can help you solve one specific problem." As the team members put it, they wanted viewers to understand they'd just been "ABM'ed."

Results: This efficiently aggressive approach generated serious results. More than 50% of monthly content downloads on Snowflake's site were driven by dedicated, collaborative 1:1 ABM campaigns. With more than 200,000 unique visitors every month, targeted display ads at just the top 1,000 accounts were responsible for half of those engagements.

What's even more impressive is that of the 1,000 campaigns Snowflake was running, there wasn't a single form or piece of gated content to be found. Instead, the team became master retargeters, building credibility with the audience before driving viewers to more traditional conversion actions, such as demonstrations or free trials.

Another metric of success for the Snowflake team? Quarterly business review invitations for the department. QBRs are where sales directors break out the book of business, showing their previous quarter's successes and sharing their commitments for the coming quarter. The ABM team's presence at these reviews affirms the real value the program is delivering for the company.

WHERE THEY ARE (B2B 2.0)

Snowflake's rivalry between B2B transformation and demand generation grew into mutual respect and common ground as both departments expanded in size. The game changed when the departments came to an agreement on MQA metrics and developed one measurement scorecard. Suddenly, the ABM team became a conduit, taking the hard work of content marketing, product marketing, demand gen, PR, and customer marketing and distilling it to metrics that drive business processes.

Developing a B2B scorecard based on engagement was the key to scaling Snowflake's program, with granular scoring of everything they do at the personal level. The scorecard tracks all marketing-driven engagements, from email openings to display ad clicks to content downloads to trade show attendees and more. Capturing and turning such data into numbers the whole organization understands drives Snowflake's hiring and regional placements and account selections as well as marketing's relationship with the finance team and executive board.

The Snowflake team members can confidently stake their careers on account-centric campaigns. The concept is no longer a buzzword, but a driver of major organizational results. For a marketing department that never was comfortable doing things the traditional way, the new and better way to do B2B has been the gateway to a new world of trying innovation and measuring success.

SIGSTR - GETTING PERSONAL, ONE CHILDREN'S MOVIE AT A TIME

> Sigstr is a relationship marketing platform that turns the billions of 1:1 emails sent every year into powerful brand engagements and practical relationship intelligence. With integrations into the leading CRMs, MAPs and Marketing Technologies, Sigstr helps companies get more out of their employee email by turning it into a channel that understands and engages their most important audiences. Leading brands like AT&T, Amazon, SendGrid, Terminus, and Yext are using Sigstr to amplify the value of every email their employees send. Visit www.sigstr.com to learn more or connect with Sigstr on Twitter, Facebook or LinkedIn.

WHERE THEY WERE (STATUS QUO)

Reality check: there isn't a universe of unlimited leads just sitting there for marketers to reach their hands out, pluck from, and hand off to sales to close. Even if it seems like your customer base is "everyone," you simply can't deliver a personalized, human experience without shrinking your universe first.

That's the lesson software startup Sigstr learned, and it's what led them to greatness. Sigstr's technology is almost universal: you've almost certainly been the recipient of an email to all@yourcompany.com that says, "Hey everyone, please update your email signatures to include this display ad," so that every email that goes out includes a promotional campaign. Sigstr's technology allows marketers to do that automatically, but with dozens or hundreds of simultaneous promotional banners.

Given that every B2B company sends emails, it seemed logical that Sigstr's Ideal Customer Profile was every B2B company. At the end of the day, though, Sigstr knew that in order to tell better stories that would resonate with people on an individual level, they had to tighten up their ICP as much as they could.

WHERE THEY WENT (ABM 1.0)

As a venture-backed company with really big revenue targets to hit, Sigstr needed to get in front of the major players in the industry. In fact, their very first account-centric program was aimed at 11 people from just one huge account.

The Sigstr team learned a few things with that first program. First, they learned how to foster direct relationships with future customers by creating a custom URL and personalized landing pages that led targets to engage with account executives. Second, they learned that they loved getting personal and treating accounts like individuals. The process was exciting, and even though they didn't land that account, they made it deep enough in the buying cycle to apply their lessons on a larger scale.

To focus their efforts on demonstrating their value to the right people to reach their aggressive revenue goals, Sigstr filtered their total addressable market through three ICP criteria: geographics, firmographics, and technographics.

GEOGRAPHICS

With customers all around the world, it was apparent that Sigstr needed to pick accounts that would allow their territory-based sales reps to efficiently meet with as many future customers as possible. They first took all of the major markets that were assigned to their sales reps and drew a 50-mile radius around it. They then took that information and made lists of companies that were headquartered there.

FIRMOGRAPHICS

Sigstr has never been afraid to go big, and they soon began to scale their efforts up from one company to 100. Again, they decided to make personalized landing pages for each of the accounts on their list, and they learned something new again: creating 100 landing pages takes as long as the exact runtime of the film Zootopia, which the team had playing on the TV in the conference room where they gathered to make the sites.

Of course, they had to get their list of 100 companies from somewhere, so Sigstr relied on firmographic data to find their largest targets.

A key firmographic criteria was the number of employees at a company. Sigstr looked at all the companies located on their list of zip codes and removed all the ones with fewer than 250 employees. For your organization, employee count might not matter so much, so you might try to filter your firmographic criteria by things like annual revenue, number of branches, how old or young the company is, and so on.

TECHNOGRAPHICS

Sigstr reviewed their customer base and found that the ones using their marketing automation or CRM integrations were stickier and had larger contract values—*DING!* That's an ideal customer! Recognizing the importance of this technographic criteria, they were able to dramatically reduce the size of their list by using the criteria as a filter.

After showing success with 100 accounts, Sigstr stepped it up a notch again. This time, they applied account-based thinking to 1000 accounts, operationalizing sales and marketing around new technology that made it easier to scale. This time, instead of building 1000 landing pages (that's ten Zootopias), Sigstr took accounts to a Drift conversation landing page that recognized the user's IP address and connected them with an account exec. Even though Sigstr couldn't know everything about every account anymore, they could still focus on bringing humans together. That was the core component of their account-based strategy.

WHERE THEY ARE (B2B 2.0)

Sigstr took an aggressive account-based approach to become legit players in their category. They went from having an ideal customer that theoretically could have been any company in the world to creating personalized experiences for a tight list of about 2,000 companies. While it required a lot of work and a lot of time poring over data and spreadsheets, having a clear idea of what an ideal customer looked like allowed Sigstr to be much more efficient with their marketing.

Making human connections has helped Sigstr tell its story and demonstrate its value. With a smaller list to work from, they're able to get specific and build relationships that extend beyond the brand. Narrowing their focus to a tighter ICP helped Sigstr increase their average customer size from 150 employees to 850 in just one year. Looks like the Sigstr universe is only expanding from here.

TERMINUS - ESCAPE FROM SPREADSHEET ISLAND

Founded in 2014, Terminus is the leader of the account-based movement. We help our customers transform B2B marketing by focusing sales and marketing resources on the best-fit, most-likely-to-buy segments of their addressable market. Our platform empowers marketing teams to easily build, operate, and measure scalable account-based initiatives that drive quality growth. We serve hundreds of B2B organizations such as Salesforce, GE, Verizon, 3M, and CA Technologies to provide the technology and expertise that produce exceptional results. Find out more at Terminus.com.

WHERE WE WERE (STATUS QUO)

You might think a company that specializes in account-based marketing would be doing ABM perfectly from the get-go. You might also think a company that wrote the first book on account-based marketing would have a highly efficient process to target the right customers, activate sales with excellent engagement data, and measure campaign success in real time.

If you thought that, you thought wrong.

If you thought that, you thought wrong.

The story of Terminus is not much different than the story of many organizations going from status quo to B2B 2.0. Our journey to great marketing was full of false starts and surprises as we learned from our own campaigns and customer feedback to make incremental improvements.

Let's go back to the beginning. We admit it: We were a lead-based organization. One of our first forays into better B2B (or ABM as we called it in the early days) was the infamous Terminus 500, in which marketing selected a list of who we thought would be the best customers to target. At the time, sales had a quarterly goal of creating 450 opportunities, so 500 accounts seemed like the perfect number to help them out. Did marketing align with sales on these accounts? Not at all, but with our focus on inbound, we were sure our quantity metrics would lead to a whole lot of wins.

Long story painfully short, sales didn't care. We hadn't selected accounts that did anything for them. Marketing quickly realized that celebrating vanity numbers wasn't going to get us anywhere, and first and foremost, we had to align with sales around their goals.

WHERE WE WENT (B2B 1.0)

Let's tell the story of how we ended up marooned on Spreadsheet Island.

It started with marketing opening the conversation with sales about how best to support both of them hitting their numbers. We understood the goal of creating those 400 to 600 opportunities, and both departments were speaking the same language, meeting regularly, and opening the lines of communication. In practice, though, some misunderstanding persisted about how exactly marketing would get them there.

Our next strategic shift was using a fit/intent/engagement model to tier all 6,500 accounts in our total addressable market. This model gave us about 200 accounts per quarter where we focused the majority of our resources, engaging mainly with account-based advertising and sales outreach. We had the false notion that sales also would focus on those 200 accounts, not grasping the difficulty of creating 400 opportunities from a small list.

The way marketing was activating sales with data was even more inefficient. And that's how we arrived at Spreadsheet Island. Every Friday, the Terminus marketing ops team worked from home, downloading spreadsheets from our predictive tools, intent tools, CRM, and marketing automation. They consolidated all the information manually, then uploaded it to Salesforce to create a list of engaged accounts for sales to look at.

It was a good-faith effort by marketing, and we were starting to understand meaningful engagement, but the process was long and mostly ineffective. A signal might come in on Monday, but it wouldn't enter the system until the end of the day Friday, and wouldn't be actionable until after the weekend. The lists were static, and marketing was leaving often inexperienced salespeople to decipher them. It was impossible to activate sales in real time with these giant reports.

Measuring the success of our campaigns also proved difficult. We were using a tool at the time, but didn't have anything resembling an engagement scorecard, so measurement could occur only at the end of every quarter. If the marketers' goal was the number of influenced accounts, they were flying blind until they could look retroactively at how close they came to hitting their numbers.

> Our ABM was superficial; we would run the same Terminus ad across all accounts and refresh it every four to six weeks. It was certainly better than the misaligned Terminus 500, but we still weren't equipped to support the numbers that sales needed.

We were calling our approach account-based, but not getting amazing results. Sales wanted air cover on all their accounts, not just marketing's list of 200. Our ABM was superficial; we would run the same Terminus ad across all accounts and refresh it every four to six weeks. It was certainly better than the misaligned Terminus 500, but we still weren't equipped to support the numbers that sales needed.

WHERE WE ARE (B2B 2.0)

The Terminus transition to the dynamic B2B program we're running today started by looking at our pain points and customer feedback to build a better process. We needed a better way to target, going from static to dynamic and getting away from spreadsheets. We needed a better process to engage across multiple channels, not just serving the same digital ad. We needed a better solution to activate sales than sending them a mammoth report. And we needed a scorecard to measure so our CRO and CMO could see how our program was performing.

> Terminus SDRs are responsible for just 100 accounts, a number that marketing is equipped to support to maximize every opportunity.

To improve our targeting, we reprioritized around fit first. We knew we had to go after more than 200 accounts, but there weren't enough accounts showing the big three factors of fit, intent, and engagement to expand our list. By starting with fit, we could target 1,500 accounts for each quarterly program. Then we could use intent along with firmographics for deeper levels of account insights to make more personal and resonant messages. Now we're able to look weekly at how companies engage, dynamically moving them in and out of different marketing programs and investing more resources when they show more engagement. Terminus SDRs are responsible for just 100 accounts, a number that marketing is equipped to support to maximize every opportunity.

We stopped just doing ads and started a multi-channel messaging approach. Whether an account is in a larger list or a 1:1 group, Terminus orchestrates across account-based display, advertising, LinkedIn, paid social, retargeting, email, direct mail, and more. It's a surround-sound messaging strategy

ABM *is* B2B.

designed to move each account to a higher level of 1:1 conversation.

At the same time that accounts engage, sales receives alerts without having to consult a dense report. SDRs are activated to have more valuable conversations because they can see exactly what content generates engagement and which plays to run next.

Our measurement also has gone to the next level. We developed an ABM scorecard that lets us compare how accounts in a particular program are doing against engagement metrics, pipeline progression, and revenue. We can compare the general population to our target accounts to see which touches are worth our investment and which resources can be diverted elsewhere.

Rescued from Spreadsheet Island, Terminus is sailing the smooth seas of predictable demand. Instead of deploying all ads at once or sending 150 pieces of direct mail at a time once a quarter, we can see who is engaging and who hasn't had an opportunity created to make weekly adjustments.

A few years ago, it was impossible to think about doing targeted and personalized campaigns for more than 200 accounts. Now, with a repeatable process in place and the technology platform to support it, Terminus is running 2,000 accounts with the capacity to go even bigger.

A few years ago, it was impossible to think about doing targeted and personalized campaigns for more than 200 accounts. Now, with a repeatable process in place and the technology platform to support it, Terminus is running 2,000 accounts with the capacity to go even bigger.

We needed a framework to help us better target, engage, activate, and measure. So we created one.

Target. Engage. Activate. Measure. Wonder if we can spell something with those initials?

TEAM. Boom!!!

So what did we learn?

We learned that dedicated teams of extraordinary marketers and sales pros can take everyday businesses, no matter what the size, to new heights. They are brave enough to challenge the status quo, crush vanity metrics, and embrace business outcomes. They are defying the odds, knowing that what sounds impossible or even impractical today may well be the norm tomorrow.

The question for you is: What are you waiting for?

If these stories inspire you, and we hope they do, it's time to dig into the TEAM Framework. This will guide you step by step on how to get started and give you the confidence that you can make a big change, too!

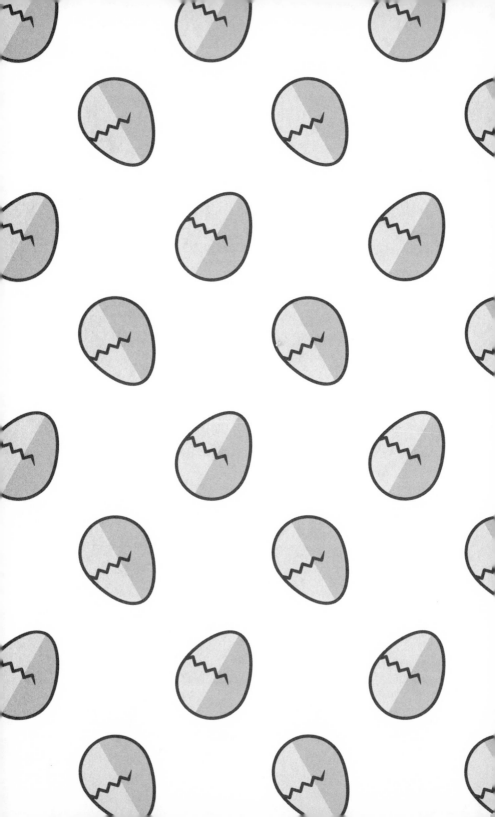

THE TEAM FRAMEWORK

THIS IS WHAT YOU HAVE BEEN WAITING FOR

You may not realize it, but you're reading a language book right now. It's no different than a Spanish textbook or a guide to common Greek sayings.

The good news is that unlike a stranger in a strange land, you're probably starting this adventure with a solid understanding of the fundamentals of account-based marketing. At least, we're assuming you are. If not, there's an earlier book about ABM that you might want to check out. We are not above inserting shameless plugs wherever we can.

In the short time since we wrote the first book on ABM, the concept has gone from a buzzword to a business trend. It's the first strategic evolution in B2B marketing since inbound. But you probably know that, and you know the basic tenets of ABM: Sell to the people most likely to buy from you. Cultivate personal relationships with your customers. Land and expand to generate more revenue. Lather, rinse, and repeat.

Where you might need a little help is in translating an overall high-level ABM strategy into actionable steps that you can take every day to work toward your goals. We have worked with hundreds of companies on implementing and executing ABM programs, and we've seen the positive results when a simple framework is applied to the practice.

A framework helps organize your thinking and get your marketing, sales, customer success, and executive teams all on the same page, all the time.

> **"Most organizations initially adopt an account-based strategy to improve critical business results, such as pipeline efficiency, retention, expansion, and customer lifetime value. Most organizations we surveyed saw some improvement right away (e.g., increased engagement in target accounts) and realized improvement over time for other results (e.g., increases to ACV and LTV).**

In a recent report, the TOPO research and advisory firm identified that an account-based go-to-market strategy delivers key results that traditional GTM can't.

Here's an abstract from the report:

"Most organizations initially adopt an account-based strategy to improve critical business results, such as pipeline efficiency, retention, expansion, and customer lifetime value. Most organizations we surveyed saw some improvement right away (e.g., increased engagement in target accounts) and realized improvement over time for other results (e.g., increases to ACV and LTV)."

"Comparing account-based to a traditional go-to-market (GTM) approach, we found that respondents overwhelmingly indicated an account-based approach is superior (see graph). Even sales cycle, the least likely result to improve, was better for 65% of respondents."

"The results also highlight the measurement challenges organizations face, particularly in the first year of account-based adoption. In the first year, 49% of companies were not able to say if their Account-based initiatives delivered a better ROI, a figure that dropped to only 8% for companies with more than 24 months of account-based experience."

ABM is a language, and everyone in your organization needs to be fluent. Welcome to your ABM Rosetta Stone.

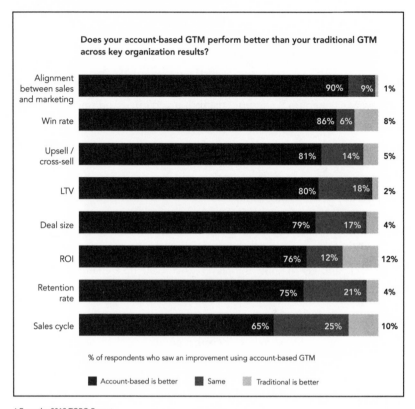

Does your account-based GTM perform better than your traditional GTM across key organization results?

Category	Account-based is better	Same	Traditional is better
Alignment between sales and marketing	90%	9%	1%
Win rate	86%	6%	8%
Upsell / cross-sell	81%	14%	5%
LTV	80%	18%	2%
Deal size	79%	17%	4%
ROI	76%	12%	12%
Retention rate	75%	21%	4%
Sales cycle	65%	25%	10%

% of respondents who saw an improvement using account-based GTM

■ Account-based is better ■ Same ▨ Traditional is better

* From the 2019 TOPO Report

INTRODUCING THE TEAM FRAMEWORK

Fans of late 1990s NBA basketball (and we know that's a lot of you) probably saw the legendary starting lineup intros for the Chicago Bulls. The stadium lights would dim dramatically, the sound system would play the first few notes of the Alan Parsons Project's Sirius, and the crowd would lose its collective mind. And that was before Scottie Pippen was even announced!

We get just as amped whenever we present our TEAM. All the lessons we learned through implementing our own ABM strategies and watching our customers succeed with their own groundbreaking uses of ABM gave us the insights to organize what we were doing into four essential components. As you'll see in a bit, ABM is a life cycle strategy, and these four components will be there for you every step of the journey.

We call it the TEAM Framework.

This framework provides a simple, execution-focused method for accelerating revenue generation, aligning marketing and sales, and improving critical acquisition and retention metrics.

It addresses the core functional areas of a modern B2B marketing organization: targeting, engagement, activation, and measurement against revenue-oriented key performance indicators.

As we introduce the framework that will be the basis for your entire ABM strategy, we encourage you to go Bulls-style with it: Dim the lights, play a hype track, and get to know the players that make up a championship B2B marketing strategy.

If you are wondering which component of the TEAM Framework is Michael Jordan, they all are! Yes, the system is that good.

Aaaaaaaand now, ladies and gentlemen, from the brains of Terminus to the world of B2B, here's the starting lineup for your . . . TEAM Framework!

The TEAM acronym stands for Target, Engage, Activate, and Measure. These factors bring marketing, sales, and customer success. Your go-to-market teams get aligned with common KPIs and finally speak the same language.

Let's dig into it.

TARGET!

Any good account-based program starts with targeting the right accounts by creating a focused list of those that are best-fit. These are folks you identify as being most likely to buy from you, based on a certain criteria.

You may see target and immediately think of net-new accounts. That's fair, because acquisition is still vital to your success with ABM, but it's not the only application of targeting. Your best-fit accounts might be in your pipeline already, or among your existing customers. Once you identify your ideal customer profile, the opportunities to target are limitless.

ENGAGE!

This is all about getting your message in front of every decision-maker in your target accounts. The good news is you're already practicing engagement tactics that are used in an ABM strategy, such as emails, webinars, and advertising. You'll be applying them several layers deeper.

ABM requires engagement on a more personalized level, with messaging that's tailored to individual roles within an account at different decision-making stages. You'll be coordinating across all your channels and mixing in some new techniques to develop a sort of surround-sound marketing that reaches the right people as early as possible.

ACTIVATE!

Cozy up together, marketing and sales teams. This is where departments mix, and revenue soars. Activation is all about triggering personalized sales outreach to the right people, at the right accounts, at the right time.

When you're focused on the same accounts, it's much easier for sales to prioritize targets by using account-level engagement data and intent signals.

MEASURE!

Those metrics you're using to define the success of your marketing program? Scrap 'em. You'll be adopting brand-new metrics that focus on account penetration and your targets' progression throughout the customer life cycle. And you'll be measuring all the time.

Come to think of it, you'll be TEAM-ing all the time. This framework is not designed to be applied linearly. The letters are in that order because, well, the MEAT Framework just doesn't sound as appealing. TEAM is an ever-evolving feedback loop that lets you continually reprioritize your targets, update your engagement tactics, and activate sales with new insights from measurement. This is how you learn and grow as an organization. Like the greatest basketball teams, this TEAM shares the focus and moves in a dynamic way. And it wins, a lot.

THE TEAM FRAMEWORK

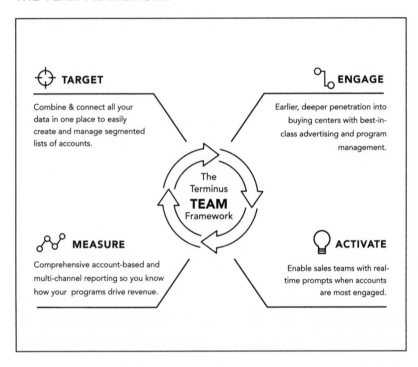

B2B IS FOR LIFE...CYCLE

At its core, account-based marketing is a life-cycle strategy. The TEAM Framework exists to breathe new life into the familiar core revenue-generating strategies you use as accounts go through the three distinct phases of their life cycle: acquisition, acceleration, and expansion.

ABM *is* **B2B.**

A simpler version (download it at terminus.com/ABMisB2B):

A more detailed version (download it at terminus.com/ABMisB2B):

ABM PLAYBOOK

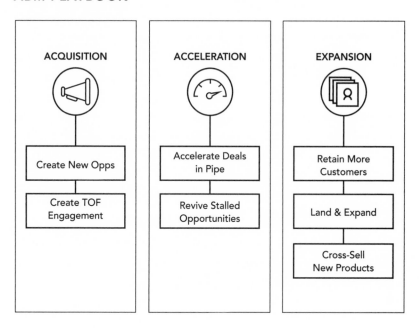

For demand-generation marketers out there giving us the side-eye now, you read that right: We're going way beyond acquisition. In fact, applying the TEAM Framework helps impact revenue no matter where a customer happens to be. Get excited.

Your organization already might be applying ABM principles to the three phases with varying degrees of success. We talked about that earlier in the B2B Maturity Curve section. No two organizations are identical when it comes to how and why they need to adopt ABM. Let's touch briefly on each phase of the life cycle so you can think through where you to apply ABM first and what impact it can have on your ability to drive quality growth.

ACQUISITION

We talk about ABM being much more than an acquisition strategy, but this is still the most common phase that marketers are invested in. It makes sense, because it's hard to accelerate an account you haven't acquired.

Taking your acquisition strategy from good to great is a matter of bringing better accounts into your pipeline. The TEAM Framework gives you better insight into the accounts you should go after and changes the conversation from obsessing over leads to measuring meaningful engagement. If you're struggling to identify accounts that are ready for sales outreach, or sales teams are telling you that the accounts you're sending them aren't useful, start here with the TEAM Framework.

PIPELINE VELOCITY

What do you do with accounts already in your pipeline? Accelerate those bad boys! The biggest challenge most companies face isn't lead volume; it's pipeline conversion. We'll quote our favorite eye-opening Forrester statistic again : Fewer than 1% of B2B leads turn into customers.

Why are all those leads getting stuck in pipelines like a bottle cap down the sink? The reason probably is that your engagement efforts aren't reaching the right decision-makers, or your sales and marketing teams are out of sync. Even if your pipes are iced up and you're in win-back mode, a little TEAM Framework magic can coordinate your messaging efforts and get the velocity flowing again.

EXPANSION

Once you acquire a customer, marketing should be enabled to focus resources efficiently on expansion to drive customer retention, land-and-expand opportunities, and cross-selling during the renewal period. That's right: Marketers should be doing this.

We know it's been difficult for B2B marketers to justify diverting resources away from acquisition and toward expansion. However, a pure ABM strategy doesn't draw a line in the sand that separates these parts of the life cycle. ABM aims to make efficient use of every marketing minute and dollar, so it can be applied confidently and comfortably wherever you need it.

Acquisition, acceleration, and expansion are the phases where ABM directly helps drive revenue goals. Once you've identified where your problem areas are, you can home in on incremental improvements in whatever stage can drive the most business outcome.

Now that you've met the TEAM Framework and started thinking about where to apply it, let's dive as deep as we can into what's possible with each TEAM player.

TARGET: CREATING YOUR IDEAL CUSTOMER PROFILE

There's an old Steve Martin joke that goes, "The secret to becoming a millionaire is to start with a million dollars." If you've never done ABM before, it can feel the same way. The secret to targeting the right accounts is figuring out ...the right accounts to target!

According to the 2019 TOPO account-based benchmark research, organizations with a strong ideal customer profile achieve 68% higher account win rates. The ICP identifies the characteristics of accounts that are more likely to become valuable customers. It is a critical element of an strategy that separates top-performing account-based organizations from their peers. "More than 80% of the most successful account-based organizations believe they have a strong ICP versus 42% of other organizations."

Winning in B2B is now a game of inches, not feet. It starts with effective, data-driven, dynamic

> According to the 2019 TOPO account-based benchmark research, organizations with a strong ideal customer profile achieve 68% higher account win rates.

targeting built on new types of account data that you can act on immediately, not tomorrow or next week.

Your ICP is a precise profile of the companies who are the best fit for your product or service, as you determined. We can't tell you what your ICP criteria are, because every company occupies a different place in the industry and market. What we can tell you is that nailing your ICP is the key to success by focusing marketing and sales resources on the right accounts.

You might recognize the term total addressable market, which is every company in the conceivable universe that you could sell to. To do B2B right, you do not want to sell to all of them! As opposed to lead-based B2B marketing, which welcomes all potential customers to the pipeline, ABM says it's necessary to ignore a large percentage of your TAM in order to find the rich account nuggets you can mine for gold over and over again.

What does Total Addressable Market mean?

Your TAM is made up of all the accounts you could possibly sell to. This is the entire revenue opportunity your product or service potentially could earn based on your current set of products and/or services. In a B2B account-based strategy, we translate this to the number of accounts we could sell to.

What does Ideal Customer Profile mean?

The ICP defines the firmographic, environmental, and behavioral attributes of accounts expected to become a company's most valuable customers.

Your ICP is the set of characteristics or attributes present in companies that will become your most valuable customers. These can be firmographic, such as the size or industry of the company (for example, larger than 500 employees); environmental, such as the organization or infrastructure of the company (for example, using a certain type of network software); or behavioral, such as activities tied to the company (for example, hiring network operations engineers).

ABM *is* **B2B.**

How are TAM and ICP different?

Your TAM is the total number of accounts that could buy your product or service ever. But just because a company could buy your product doesn't mean that you should invest valuable time and resources in marketing to it.

Your resources are scarce. Even if you sell an SaaS tool, there is a cost in people and resources for every customer you bring on. Someone must help manage your customers and create new features to keep them happy, and you need support staff to manage those people.

Although your product could serve an infinite number of people, that doesn't mean you have the resources to handle that volume. The point is that you should view your product as a scarce resource, no matter how much actually is available.

The point is that you should view your product as a scarce resource, no matter how much actually is available.

This is where your ICP comes into play. A TAM is a more idealistic number of accounts, while an ICP is the realistic number of accounts that you should focus on. These are the accounts that are easiest to convert into opportunities, have the shortest sales cycles, and become the happiest customers.

Keep in mind that you probably won't target your entire ICP at the same time. It would be great if you could, but most companies don't have the resources to do that. If you define your ICP and find that you do have the budget and bandwidth to target the entire list of accounts, you were probably too restrictive in defining it.

Here's an example of an ICP for a hypothetical project-management tool that your company sells:

Industry: B2B SaaS companies

Location: U.S. or Canada

Size: engineering team of 15 people

Annual revenue: at least $20 million

Customer base: mid-market and enterprise businesses that require dependable release schedules

This narrows it down and starts to paint a clean picture of who your sales efforts should focus on. Perhaps more importantly, it eliminates a ton of companies who would waste your time.

Again, it's up to you to compile the important criteria. But that doesn't mean you have to guess. You already have the data at your disposal to craft an initial ICP, whether you're an established company with thousands of customers or just getting off the ground looking for your first few dozen.

For larger companies, start with customer data in your customer relationship management, or CRM. Find the most successful ones and build an ICP that's modeled after what an ideal customer already looks like. Start by pulling a list of the accounts with the highest deal sizes. What do they have in common? You can look at specific installed technologies to give you an even more complete picture.

Next, pull a list of all your renewals or repeat buyers during the past year, and do the same thing. What do they have in common? You can compare this list with companies that didn't renew and see what makes these accounts different. Wherever a trend emerges, that's a shining symbol of an attribute that should go in your ICP.

If you're a younger company or an established company moving into a new market, you might not have a wealth of proprietary baseline data to pull from. In this case, your ICP will be based on characteristics and require market research to fill in the criteria.

No matter how you craft your ICP, do not go at it alone with your marketing team. Sales and customer success must be involved from the beginning so the common language is defined and understood. Once you're done—though you're never really done, because ABM is a continuous feedback loop—make sure to circulate your ICP across your organization so everyone is aligned as #OneTeam.

TARGET: GETTING A 360-DEGREE VIEW OF YOUR ACCOUNTS

Imagine sitting down for a meal at a nice restaurant, and before you even look at the menu, the server brings out your dinner. The chef spent hours preparing it, and it looks great—except that you're allergic to half of what's on the plate. You're probably never going back to that restaurant, right? Well, when marketers build campaigns without knowing what their future customers want, they're dishing up meals that will probably go uneaten.

For you to succeed, you must meet your target audience members where they are, which requires knowing everything about them. That's what we call getting a 360-degree view of an account.

To do this, you need to build an account intelligence database from lots of different data sources. In fact, account intelligence in ABM uses some of the most cutting-edge data techniques of any marketing discipline.

Getting started can be easy. To build a 360-degree account view, you need to look at two types of account data: fit and behavior.

Fit is the most straightforward. It comprises firmographic features of companies, such as their size, industry, technographic profile, and organizational structure. These are characteristics of each company that make it a good fit for what you're selling. Basically, this is where you match future customers to your ICP.

You can assemble a fit profile on your own, or use an AI-assisted/predictive fit-scoring tool to help determine which characteristics have the strongest correlation with your past sales success and generate a fit score for each account in your CRM.

Then dive into behavioral data. This is information about what the account has done, and it falls into three buckets:

Intent data: How the account is behaving in the market and what the account is searching for across the Internet. You can get this data from a variety of providers.

For example, if you sell project-managing software for IT teams, your future customers in the market for a solution might search for articles about project management, agile, kanban work scheduling, and so on. An intent data solution can alert you to accounts that are researching these topics, whether or not they've ever visited your company's website.

That last part is the game-changer. In traditional B2B marketing, you're often at the mercy of visitors filling out a form on your website or visiting your booth at a trade show to get any information about them. In the ABM or better B2B world, you no longer need to wait for those customers to come to you.

Engagement data: How much an account has interacted with your company through your website, marketing, and sales activities.

As you'll learn, not all engagement is created equal in ABM. How you define meaningful engagement will be up to you, but such data can be critical in getting to know your customers because they've already expressed an interest in you.

Engagement data measures how much an account has interacted with you. This might mean not at all (or not at all according to your meaningful engagement criteria). No engagement does not necessarily make for a bad target, however. In many cases, you may choose to target high-fit, high-intent, but low-engagement accounts to ensure that your brand is front and center.

Relationship data: How an account has interacted with your sales or success team in the past.

These data measure the depth, breadth, and quality of the relationship between your company and a target account. This is yet another example of ABM as a life-cycle strategy. You can use relationship data to retarget accounts that have moved past acquisition and are stuck in the pipeline, or select current customers who would be best-fit for cross-sell and upsell opportunities.

To gather these feeds, you might need to add to your tech stack. Often, however, you already have the information in your existing stack and simply need to organize better.

TARGET: BUILDING YOUR ACCOUNT LISTS

Your ABM strategy is only as good as the accounts you're going after. Sirius Decisions found that 91% of teams doing ABM closed larger deals from their target accounts than from non-target accounts. That's why it's so important to get your target account lists right.

> **Your ABM strategy is only as good at the accounts you're going after. Sirius Decisions found that 91% of teams doing ABM close larger deals from their target accounts than from non-target accounts.**

As a marketer, you're probably familiar with segmentation. Anytime you have a go-to-market strategy for a group of accounts, that's a unique segment. B2C marketers, who sell directly to consumers, do this all the time with creative campaigns that feel as if they're targeting a specific person. Segmentation has always been different in B2B, where the emphasis hasn't been on high-touch, individualized tactics.

From the perspective of *ABM is B2B*, creating a list of specific accounts helps marketing and sales teams prioritize the hottest accounts, tailor messaging to those segments, and run more personal campaigns. You won't invite every account to an intimate webinar, but you will make the most of your messaging tactics when you guarantee yourself maximum impact.

There are three ways to segment dynamically within ABM: one-to-many, one-to-few, and one-to-one.

In one-to-many, you're targeting a group of accounts with similar characteristics based on firmographic data, such as industry or company size, or on intent data, such as companies that are researching similar products online. This is almost the same as traditional B2B marketing, except now you have a named account list.

> **There are three ways to segment dynamically within ABM: one-to-many, one-to-few, and one-to-one.**

For example, you might decide to send email or direct mail targeted to all the financial services companies in your target account list. You're not qualifying these accounts as high-priority, hence the more general one-to-many approach. Maybe they meet only a few of your ICP criteria but have shown intent to buy. You wouldn't want to ignore them, but you also wouldn't want to waste valuable resources on fish that might not bite.

With one-to-few, you should get more personal with your messaging and leverage engagement data to achieve that level of personalization. In the right industry, these accounts might be a bit off from checking every box of your ICP, for example, but have too few employees. They're close, though, and they've shown intent.

Either way, you now have a smaller group of accounts to go after with the one-to-many approach. There are several ways to create this list, and more creative tactics to show them you care.

For example, you could look at engagement metrics, such as accounts with website visits to high-value pages, and deliver relevant ads to the top 100 most-engaged accounts. Or try what we've done, and follow up with personalized, direct-mail cupcakes. Who doesn't like cupcakes?

It's important to note that accounts are never stuck in one place. A one-to-many account can transition easily to a one-to-few account and beyond. ABM makes sure that you'll be prepared with new, unique messaging tactics that are appropriate for the segment list you're targeting. In other words, if an account moves into the one-to-few list, your relationship will grow in momentum naturally. The same holds true for accounts that cross over the other way, so you'll never be too pushy.

The ultimate high-value accounts get the one to-one treatment. This is where you spend more resources and budget to tailor your content, but the payoff is much higher. The reason is that you've segmented to discover who is ripe for your solution, right now.

For example, imagine running a one-to-one ad that takes your future customer to a targeted landing page, which displays the company's colors and offers content specifically about the company and how you can solve its problems. You have a dedicated team serving this account with regular, relevant content. Suddenly, those cupcakes become steakhouse dinners, and you're opening networking doors to industry peers that happen to be your clients. It's a highly effective way of engaging your high-value accounts.

When you have a complete view of your best-fit accounts, including their intent and engagement insights, you can continually slice and dice your lists for better targeting and personalization of your message.

Again, this is not something you do just one time. You need to continually update your target lists as new data come in, and as existing accounts move in and out of your original segments. You want to understand how your target accounts as a whole are progressing through the buyer's journey, so they can receive different, more relevant messaging as they move into a new segment.

Remember that the first step in segmenting is deciding which of your accounts correspond to which business value. Once you know that, you can apply one of the three segmentation strategies and create personalized experiences that your current and future customers will love.

ENGAGE: DEFINING MEANINGFUL ENGAGEMENT

Let's start by pouring one out for MQLs. The marketing-qualified lead had a good run. So many forms were filled out on your website, and so many potential customers were passed from marketing to sales based on this one-size-fits-all trigger. Ah, the good old days . . . or maybe not. The TEAM Framework puts MQLs out to pasture because in the world of ABM, you never sell to a lead, but always to an account. That means a new performance indicator must be used to measure success, and it's called engagement.

Ah, but not all engagement is created equal! How do you separate the good stuff from the fluff? It comes down to the basic commandment that we learned from running thousands of ABM campaigns for companies of all sizes: When we talk about engagement, we should talk about **quality** over **quantity.**

> **Meaningful engagement is some aggregation of known and anonymous data, but the criteria for what's meaningful will be different for every organization.**

With the ABM = B2B mindset, you must look at how all stakeholders (i.e., the entire buying committee) are engaging with your brand, even if they've never filled out a form on your website. This has become easier to track with advancements in marketing technology. It's still a massive strategic shift over scoring individual leads.

Meaningful engagement is some aggregation of known and anonymous data, but the criteria for what's meaningful will be different for every organization. As a marketer, you need to show that you're creating engagement among your target accounts week over week. That way, you can alert the account owner when a target is spiking, meaning more visits from that account to your website or landing page.

If you don't have many customers yet, or you sell only one product or offer one service line, meaningful engagement could be 10 high-value website visits from four people in an account. If you can turn website visits into opportunities, then by all means, make it as simple as possible.

Not all visits are the same, so focusing on high-value page activity could mean focusing on the right accounts from the get-go.

If you sell multiple products or have a high-traffic website, you might want to go deeper than website visits. Here, you can use a slightly more complex model based on engagement spikes. It might look something like this:

**number of unique visitors from a
target account to your website**

+

number of campaign responses per account

Campaign responses can be content downloads, trade show visits, webinar views, and similar things. These types of spikes are strong indicators that stakeholders at your account are ramping up their interest in what you're selling.

This is a powerful sign because it can be customized and adapted to changes in your business strategy. You can create more than one model to see which performs better over time.

You may ask how you fill in this model with the appropriate numbers. One way is to look into current open deals in your sales cycle and use their pre-opportunity engagement levels as a baseline. Once you understand what meaningful engagement looks like to your business, you measure the increase or decrease in your engagement metrics.

Another metric we like to track is rate of meaningful engagement, which is the percentage of target accounts that are currently engaged, based on the model of your choice.

> **The most important thing to do first is to define what engagement means to you and your organization and get consensus from your leadership team. It might take many iterations to find the one that works for your business.**

Yet another metric is the time from the first touchpoint to meaningful engagement. That's the span for converting an account from the first brand touchpoint (such as visiting a website) to a meaningful level of engagement (such as watching a customer testimonial or setting a demonstration).

The most important thing to do first is to define what engagement means to you and your organization and get consensus from your leadership team. It might take many iterations to find the one that works for your business.

Landing on the most appropriate engagement metrics doesn't necessarily mean that every account that engages is sales-ready. If you're triggering marketing campaigns or sales handoffs only after single activities, such as content downloads, your number of leads may continue to increase, but your conversions probably will go down.

This indicates that your teams don't have enough insight to build relevant campaigns to move accounts through a personalized buying process. However, if you know that a prospect is the right fit, and you can to glean insight into what it's consuming on your site, you can personalize and prioritize your outreach to increase the velocity of your buyer's journey.

As important as tracking and measuring account engagement are, it's meaningless if you aren't acting on those insights. You should have processes in place to trigger actions based on the level of engagement shown by target accounts.

To act effectively on engagement insights, you should segment account engagement and have specific programs and campaigns for each segment.

ABM *is* **B2B.**

ENGAGE: COMMUNICATING AUTHENTICALLY

The success of your ABM program hinges on how well you can be a real person. Even though you represent a brand offering a product or service, you're selling to living, breathing people at the end of the day. These real people have real lives, with places they like to go and things they like to do.

Your job as a marketer is to meet them where they are in an authentic way.

The more authentically you can communicate and the more realistic your conversations are, the more people will trust you. That's true in life, and it's certainly true in B2B marketing. We believe the marketing and sales teams that beat the odds in a crowded market do so not only because they know everything about their product, but also because they're completely in tune with their customers' wants and needs.

> **The more authentically you can communicate, and the more realistic your conversations are, the more people will trust you.**

Since ABM allows you to focus on a few accounts, you can dig deeper and know more about your customers than you could with a traditional marketing approach. You can do his one of two ways:

First, think about how you can engage future customers on their terms to become a trusted advisor.

Let's say your future customers love being on LinkedIn and Twitter, and use those platforms to share their thoughts on business and life in general. By noticing the moments when they share a story or detailed a problem they are facing, you can find a few quick links that will help them with their needs. Your response need not be complex; you could send blogs or articles that aren't from your organization. If it makes sense, you could even share a case study from a customer who is much like them, and build credibility in the process. All you have to do is show that you care and you listen.

The second way to communicate more authentically is to become a connector.

Let's say you find out that your future customers need to grow their business in a particular vertical, and you happen to know a couple of customers who have done so. It's time to play matchmaker. By introducing them to each other, you instantly build trust, not to mention a nice business bridge, and again show how much you care.

You can do this online or in person, depending on how much the business is worth to you. We organize dinners all the time where we're not acting as the hero, but just playing the role of connector. It's amazing to see where those conversations go when you get people in a room with similar stories and problems that your solution just happens to fix.

This might seem like a lot of effort, but tools can help you locate your future customers and reach them at exactly the right time. Here are a few things we do:

- Set Google alerts on the names of the companies and future customers so you are notified in real time whenever they're making news.

- Follow the key decision-makers on social media and start listening to their interests and questions. LinkedIn and Twitter can help you keep their online activity at the top of your feed.

- Here's a pro tip. Set up Google and social media alerts for your future customers' competitors. There's nothing that will blow your customers' mind in a good way like alerting them to a problem they don't yet know they have or showing them a solution that will get them ahead of what their competitors are doing.

As soon as you see your future or current customers doing anything interesting, notify them, and share something that will help them beat their competitors using your product or service. Again, case studies are your friend.

Are you ready to get real? Stop studying your own product and start making it your top priority to learn about your customers' needs. Trust us, there

ABM *is* **B2B.**

are tons of companies, many of them your competitors, who can answer any questions about their own business, but end up shouting the answers into the void because they don't know where their customers are. Your curiosity for the business landscape around you and how your customers fit into it will be what distinguishes you in the long run.

ENGAGE: ORCHESTRATING MULTICHANNEL CAMPAIGNS

Let's say you just had a baby (congrats!) and you wanted to share the happy news with friends and family. Would you send just one text to one friend and hope the news spreads? Of course not! You'd make phone calls, send emails, take adorable baby pics, post on social media, and fly balloons on your mailbox.

Well, as a B2B marketer, your product or service is your baby, and the same idea applies to ABM. Once you've crafted a perfect, personal message, you want to place it in front of your target accounts across multiple channels.

In order to maximize your effect and efficiency, you need to focus on the right channels and orchestrate outreach in a coordinated way. The goal of multichannel campaigns is to engage all relevant contacts in an account on channels they value most.

To orchestrate multichannel campaigns, first create a campaign orchestration matrix.

This will lay out:

- Which channels you plan to use, such as email, web personalization, direct mail, sales outreach, and digital advertising.
- The sales stages that an account moves through during your sales process.

When you define the sales stages, you also should define which specific triggers you'll use to launch the channel activity you've defined for each stage.

Triggers are events that you can track using your ABM platform, or with other marketing technologies that show your account has progressed to the next stage.

You can use these to launch new emails, herald ad campaigns, or ping your sales team to reach out.

For example, if you're selling to IT departments, you may use an email click and multi-page web engagement from your CTO as a trigger to send a piece of direct mail from yours to theirs. Other channels available include nurture emails, in-market events or dinners, and even specific sales scripts.

You also can orchestrate account-based advertising through sponsored content on Facebook, Twitter, LinkedIn, or a dedicated account-based advertising network.

To take it a step further, when your accounts become more engaged, you might send them to a personalized content hub. This hub is a repository of content anyone from your team can update with articles, ebooks, case study videos, or industry reports to provide a more customized experience for your best-fit and engaged accounts.

If you're looking for a neat place to start your engagement channels, here are the top five tactics, digital and physical, used by ABM marketers:

Digital channels:

- Account advertising, often best done through targeted, paid campaigns in social media.
- Web personalization, with home pages and site experiences that vary depending on who visits your site.

Human outreach, using emails sent by your account reps, not by automation software.

Physical channels:

- Field marketing, featuring events run by your company or third parties, with your outreach efforts focused on networking.

- Direct mail, which still works when you make it super personal and valuable. Who doesn't open the FedEx package?

Multichannel campaign orchestration ties into what we discussed about personalization in the targeting section. By monitoring your engagement and intent levels, you'll know when it's time to deploy more high-touch, one-to-few or one-to-one outreach on the appropriate channels

When it comes to personalization, sales teams have traditionally relied upon cursory social media research and data from form fills to gain insight on targeted individuals and accounts. But let's face it: Your sales team needs to dig deeper than "Hey, we have the same alma mater." This is where account-level engagement insights allow you to power your personalization. With this data, you'll have access to both known and anonymous contact information. You can see intent and engagement data as well as which accounts are leaning in on specific product or content pages. It's a powerful way to activate sales teams to reach these accounts, as they now have the perfect message to use.

For instance, one of the first things you might analyze is which accounts visited your site and didn't fill out a form. Which pages did they visit? What content are they searching? How can you better support them with more relevant content that may address their questions?

Multichannel campaigns are not just a great opportunity to flex your creative muscle within ABM. They've also been proven to work. One InfoTrends report found that the response rate for multichannel campaigns was 9.5%, up from 7.4% for email only. Don't risk the chance that the right person at your best-fit account happens to not check email. Be omnipresent so you can discover what works.

In ABM you win or lose as #OneTeam.

In ABM, you win or lose as #OneTeam. Don't forget to bring sales teams into the mix, and ensure their plays are integrated with your campaigns so you are always reinforcing the same messaging.Speaking of sales, let's start activating them in the next section.

ACTIVATE: ACTIVATING SALES WITH DATA AND INSIGHTS

Look around your sales department.

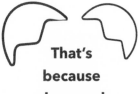

That's because salespeople are given the title of account executives.

How many of those positive attitudes and smiling faces belong to someone with the title "lead executive?"

We're guessing none.

That's because salespeople are given the title of account executives.

Giving them leads has never worked. Remember the earlier Forrester research statistic: Fewer than 1% of leads turn into customers.

But if you deliver engagement and leads in the accounts they are working on, you will be their hero. They can deliver on-the-ball service to nurture future and current customers using a lot of data and a little bit of charm.

Sales teams care about only one thing, and it isn't your marketing leads. No, they care about the accounts they need to close this month or quarter. Volume-driven demand-gen produced a fundamental gap between marketing and sales incentives. ABM, which is the new B2B, arrived just in time to close that gap.

Successful account-centric campaigns aren't only about targeting the right accounts and executing personalized cross-channel marketing programs.

That's the first part. What comes next is crucial, because if you fumble the sales handoff, all that work goes for naught.

Marketing must activate salespeople by delivering advanced account intelligence and personalization tools to help prioritize and personalize their outreach. You're creating a playbook from the common language your departments speak, driven by data to guarantee a consistent experience for accounts. Without a reliable playbook, your customers may look at you as if you grew a second head that doesn't communicate with the first.

You can do this by adopting the Next-Show-Go approach to sales intelligence. This means helping sales answer three simple questions:

- Which account do I need to take action on next?
- What engagement signals is that account showing?
- What action or play should I take based on those signals to go after this account?

Ideally, these insights are delivered directly where your sales team lives, typically in your CRM. A wise person once said, "If it's not in salesforce, it doesn't exist." For younger teams, these insights also can be delivered as a spreadsheet or set of automated emails.

So, how do you deliver this data? A good account-based platform should show activity from known and anonymous visitors, and roll it up to the account level so sales can create ranked reports based on this activity. You also can deliver engagements with other campaigns, such as one-to-one ads, email nurtures, or event registrations to complete the prioritization picture.

What does this look like in real time?

> **A good account-based platform should show activity from known and anonymous visitors, and roll it up to the account level so sales can create ranked reports based on this activity.**

Here an example of plays based on level of engagement:

If this	Then do this
Target account activity "surging" on the website	Alert the Sales rep assigned to that account
Accounts in the same location engaged	Launch an event play in that location
Target account has no activity over 30 or 60 days	Turn on an activation campaign with direct mail or targeted advertising
New best-fit accounts showing engagement	Align executive outreach to "up-level" the conversation and increase deal velocity
120 days after the deal is won	Launch a targeted advertising campaign to up-sell or cross-sell with new products and service offering, if applicable

This gives sales greater clarity on which accounts to go after next.

You can combine this information with data about exactly which topics, ideas, or concerns the folks in an account are showing interest in.

Pull live signals like most-visited URLs on your site, alongside intent data pulled from elsewhere on the web. Now you have all the relevant accounts that have a good chance of leading to sales.

Once your playbook is set up, it's time to go after the money. Sales leadership should collaborate with top reps to come up with a series of focused plays, an index of great content, and clear personalization instructions so they can start a meaningful conversation with accounts.

Your sales playbook is not the exclusive property of your sales team. Remember, it takes full organizational alignment to run ABM, and that goes for the plays during the activation phase. Sales is most heavily involved, but your marketing tactics and even the occasional cameo from your executive team will solidify a cohesive activation playbook.

Check out this 31-day orchestration plan devised by TOPO. It breaks down the tactic, who the play is intended for at the account level, and who owns the play at your organization.

Type	Activity	Audience	Owner	Notes
1-Day 1	Marketing email	All	Marketing	Announce event, feature keynote
2-Day 1	Postal	DM	Marketing	Dimensional mailer, event brochure. Drop day 1, arrive day 3-4
3-Day 8	Marketing email	All, segmented	Marketing	"Why attend?", featuring relevant speaker (by person)
4-Day 11	SDR call	Stakeholder, DM	SDR	Invite call
5-Day 11	SDR email	All	SDR	Invite email, feature relevant companies attending
6-Day 14	Exec email	Exec	Exec	Personalized invitation from CIO
7-Day 18	Marketing email	All	Marketing	"Less than two weeks!", feature VR Lounge after-party
8-Day 22	SDR call	Stakeholder, DM	SDR	Invite call
9-Day 22	SDR email	All	SDR	Personalized email, feature networking
10-Day 24	Marketing email	All	Marketing	"One week away!" message
11-Day 28	SDR email	All	SDR	"Last chance! Registration closes tomorrow! Message
12-Day 29	Marketing email	All	Marketing	"Just 4 more hours to register!" message
Day 31	Live event			

Even within this tight structure, there's always room for adjustment as you notice account movement within the Next-Show-Go model. If any of these plays inspires significantly more engagement, change your tactics to reflect the new account velocity. Likewise, if continued outreach from your account executive keeps turning colder, you'll know when to switch things up and deploy new message delivery.

This can be complex, especially if you have thousands of accounts in the pipeline. Any ABM program requires an iterative approach, such as setting up organized playbooks. If your failure to launch is the result of intimidation, start small. There's nothing wrong with looking at a single account action and manually setting up plays based on it. As you make progress and learn more, you can start building lists and launching plays to a group of accounts at a time. Once you have full intelligence, you can set up automated triggers that personalize your outreach plays to the specific accounts that meet your criteria.

But you can't do anything if you don't empower your sales team with your data. Learn about the accounts they care about and satiate their hunger for insights with the intelligence that will make them stand out for their current and future customers.

MEASURE: MEASURING THE NEW B2B FUNNEL

If you've been reading this book from the beginning, we apologize for getting redundant. If you opened up right here, good for you! You stumbled on the most important shift from traditional demand gen to account-centric programs. Here it is, for the first or the dozenth time:

B2B IS NOT ABOUT LEADS! It's about winning the accounts that you can serve the best, and that bring the highest value to your organization. And winning is a team sport!

Gosh, it feels good to get that out there. That's the kind of sentence we want to yell from a mountaintop. Try it the next time you take a hike or feel extra confident at your desk.

Because the mindset shifts in account-centric from focusing on lead volume and qualification to targeting the right accounts and progressing toward closed opportunities, the metrics used to evaluate your program change, too.

B2B IS NOT ABOUT LEADS! It's about winning the accounts that you can serve the best and that have the highest value to your organization. And winning is a team sport!

If you still use traditional funnel metrics for leads, your account-centric program will look limp and ineffective by comparison, even if it's performing amazingly.

Why is that? The truth is, it can take a little while to reap the fruits of your labor.

Organizational buy-in requires full understanding that things won't always go according to plan right out of the gate. If you, your sales team, your executives, or anyone else at your company can't play a waiting game when quantity metrics start going down, your account-based program will never get off the ground.

The new B2B funnel brings a brand-new set of metrics that give you tremendous insight into the nuances of account performance. Old-school counting of stats, such as total leads or form fills, isn't useful anymore. It's all about optimizing account-based programs by studying advanced measurements in the juicy parts of the customer journey.

Account-based marketers are responsible for revenue throughout the pipeline. As a result, you need to show not only how well you're bringing accounts in, but also how effectively you are progressing them through and generating more opportunities with current customers once you've won their business.

There are three areas of focus when measuring the success of your account-based program:

- Creating and deepening relationships with target accounts.
- Moving accounts through to desired results.
- Achieving account-based return on investment.

To see how well you're doing in these areas, start at the beginning of the new B2B funnel with your target accounts. This is the number of accounts that you selected through list-building and segmentation to target with account-based programs. The total should be static over the course of a given program, because the primary goal is to understand how much of the target account list has progressed and how much is left to close.

From there, look at relationships. These are your engaged accounts, those that have interacted with your company in some way. Most of the time, it will be through a website visit. Several account-based analytics tools can link known and anonymous contact activity on your site to individual accounts. Although site visits are often great indicators of interest, what you're really seeking is quality of the engagement. What's superficial vs. deeper and more meaningful?

One way to quantify depth of engagement is assigning a value to different types of interactions. A website visit is valuable, but it's probably less valuable than a target account viewing a webinar, which, in turn, is less valuable than attending a dinner. Developing a hierarchy of engagement is a great way to gauge your awareness and the effectiveness of your outreach.

In this new approach, you won't report on cost per lead or rates of lead conversion anymore. Instead, focus on the conversion rate from total accounts to engaged accounts, from total accounts to opportunity accounts, and from total accounts to closed accounts.

From there, accounts progress to the opportunity stage. There should be a forecasted deal value associated with each opportunity, which will help you understand your total pipeline. This is different from traditional measurement of demand generation, because the account-based approach takes the entire account's journey into consideration, not just a single lead. Measuring progress toward desired goals keeps marketing and sales aligned, because as a marketer, you have greater influence with open opportunities.

As an account moves through the stages from open opportunity to closed and even beyond, focus on new conversion metrics to understand how effective your programs are and decide where to ramp up the effort.

In this new approach, you won't report on cost per lead or rates of lead conversion anymore. Instead, focus on the conversion rate from total accounts to engaged accounts, from total accounts to opportunity accounts, and from total accounts to closed accounts.

For example, if you're targeting 100 accounts, you might be able to engage 50 of them. Of those 50 accounts, 25 might turn into opportunity, and 5 might close.

What happens after you close?

Because the approach is a life-cycle strategy, your impact on won customers can be measured, as well. Expansion, cross-sell, upsell, and advocacy are all distinct journeys customers take, and they can be measured with the same principles of engagement quality and opportunity conversion as new pipeline targets.

The new approach helps you focus on business outcomes. When you report on metrics that matter, you instantly align your organization with acting and thinking like #OneTeam that no longer cares about total leads. Let's shout it from the rooftops!

MEASURE: FORECASTING THE NEW ABM PIPELINE

Imagine you're in charge of buying gifts for your family during the holidays. Simple enough, right? What if you were handed a list of family members to shop for, and the number of names on it kept changing? You didn't plan to get anything for your second cousins. And who is Uncle Bob? The confusion would make your shopping strategy inefficient and unsuccessful.

Many companies build forecasting models for pipeline revenue that are equally chaotic. Account-based strategy can help. Unfortunately, if you're just starting, you don't have a baseline of past performance to compare with your new program.

What to do?

You can start forecasting by analyzing the previous two or three quarters of pipeline conversion rates across the entire organization, looking at your win rates and conversion rates between stages. Now you have a baseline of where you've been before. When you implement the account-based program, you can expect it to roughly equal, if not exceed, those same conversion rates.

Your second step is to analyze patterns in different conversion rates with account-centric thought to make sure you meet your established baseline. If you don't, it's a signal to reassess and figure out what went wrong. Chances are, you'll get better results with this focused approach than any spray-and-pray method deployed in the past.

Once you meet your baseline, your third step is to set future goals.

Set metrics to improve these conversion rates by certain percentage points every quarter, based on whatever your business demands. The goal of forecasting is not achieving 100% accuracy, but coming as close as possible so you have a predictable business model you can put in front of anyone and guarantee results. This includes your executive team.

MEASURE: REPORTING TO YOUR C-SUITE AND BOARD

Getting aligned on the metrics that matter in the new B2B funnel is critical, and not for the reason you may think. Yes, proper measurement is key to understanding your own program, but you're not the one who needs convincing. You already know the account-centric approach works. Your executives, on the other hand…let's just say they're not gifting this book to everyone in your marketing department.

At some point, you have to pitch your c-suite and board on an account-centric strategy. You can't go rogue and practice ABM without buy-in from the top. It's a #OneTeam approach and mindset.

If you work at a successful organization and hit your sales numbers every quarter using a more traditional approach, then good luck, young Padawan, for this will not be easy. Change is tough, especially when times are okay-to-good. That's why you must arm yourself with numbers. Develop reports as simply

> **At some point, you have to pitch your c-suite and board on an account-centric strategy. You can't go rogue and practice ABM without buy-in from the top. It's a #OneTeam approach and mindset.**

ABM *is* **B2B.**

as possible to show non-practitioners what's working and what's not with the accounts that drive your desired business outcomes.

You're an account-centric-approach evangelist, and you preach at the altar of your reporting dashboard.

It's as simple as comparing and contrasting ROI. You need to show your executives how your ABM program stacks up against other marketing initiatives. Knowing what to measure and seeing it all in one dashboard takes the guesswork out of identifying gaps within teams, and creates clarity around the problems that need attention.

What goes into this all-important executive report?

Start with the segments you're targeting. Give each target account list a name and a brief summary of the segmentation criteria you used to select the accounts, such as vertical, intent data, or engagement metrics. This helps to keep everyone on the same page about which parts of your total addressable market are driven by account-centric programs.

You can then leverage the highest-level account-based funnel, broken down by each account list as well as each strategy of acquisition, acceleration, and expansion. Be sure to include both acquisition and current customer expansion in this dashboard.

Key measurement metrics here include average contract value, win rate, sales cycle length, retention rate, and net promoter score. You want to establish baselines to see if you're improving over time, and include goals to see if you're achieving what you set out to do. This will reveal opportunities for improvement at different stages.

For example, you might have a lot of accounts in the IT vertical, but the lowest percentage of won accounts compared with other segments. You can adjust your tactics further along the funnel to create more engagement and improve your win rate.

> **TOPO predicts that organizations will begin to refocus their account-based programs around the idea of B2BCX, or customer experience. Those who crack the code of finding more insightful account intelligence, better methods of account targeting, and quicker ways to activate that intelligence will win the race.**

To highlight the effect of an account-centric B2B program, your dashboard should include a comparison of your target account pipelines to your non-target ones. That's real money!

There may be no clearer indication of the benefits of your account-centric program than being able to see your target strategy at play versus the rest of your marketing strategy, meaning your inbound and outbound accounts. Put your account-centric numbers side by side with your traditional numbers, and the results will speak for themselves. You'll see where the strategies diverge, and which plays and programs are generating the most impact.

Your goal is not to prove to your board that account-centric marketing is correct. You're simply showing how marketing can be better utilized to drive organizational goals.

When implemented correctly, ABM creates high-value engagement in the accounts you can serve the best, and your c-suite cares the most about that. Is it a better use of resources than what you're already doing? Then you can present your dashboard and your program with confidence.

The B2B buying process looks completely different than it did even a few years ago, and it's becoming continually more complex. In the past two years, the number of stakeholders involved in the purchase decision has increased 26%. The game, now played in inches rather than feet, is no longer about selling to an individual buyer. It's about building relationships with the entire organization.

TOPO predicts that organizations will begin to refocus their account-based programs around the idea of B2BCX, or customer experience. Those who crack the code of finding more insightful account intelligence, better methods of account targeting, and quicker ways to activate that intelligence will win the race.

By targeting the right accounts with the right message at the right time, you'll be able to:

- Increase pipeline among new and existing accounts.
- Improve pipeline velocity.
- Improve retention rates.
- Enhance the buyer experience.

Just remember, it starts with being able to leverage the right data in near-real time, and putting that data into action quickly. Having one centralized hub to manage it all can make a world of difference.

TEAM IS NOT JUST A FUN FRAMEWORK, IT'S A MINDSET.

Think of your sales and marketing as one unit, and pull in customer success to form a unified, go-to-market team. A winning team has the vision to answer the fundamental questions of why you do what you do and how you do it, so spend time answering these questions yourself first before you go about implementing the TEAM framework in your organization.

Give yourself permission to relax and find time to define and refine your vision of success, metrics to celebrate, and barriers to overcome to create a #OneTeam culture and TEAM framework.

We're rooting for you!

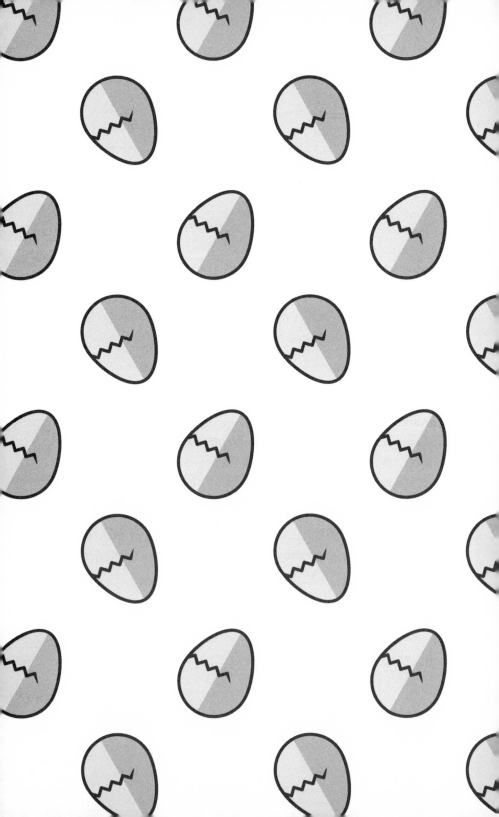

YOU CAN START TODAY

Putting the TEAM Framework into Action

If you're planning to tear down your house and rebuild it from the ground up, you need a blueprint to guide you. Otherwise, you might find yourself working from what you already know and putting walls up in the same old places, or worse, starting construction with disorganized plans and building walls of different heights.

Rethinking your B2B marketing requires the same level of precision as remodeling a home. All the parts must work together, and all the details must be accounted for. If you're like most organizations, you've never lived in a house quite like the one you're building with an account-based foundation, so the blueprints and tools you used to construct your old B2B living spaces don't apply anymore.

According to the 2019 TOPO benchmark research report, an account-based strategy requires dedicated leadership from program inception. More than two-thirds of top-performing account-based organizations now have a dedicated account-based leader. The market has caught on: 70% of those who started account-based initiatives in the past six months have dedicated leaders. In contrast, only 58% of companies that missed their account-based objectives have dedicated leadership.

> **According to the 2019 TOPO benchmark research report, an account-based strategy requires dedicated leadership from program inception.**

If B2B 2.0 is shaking up the foundation of what marketing can be, the TEAM Framework is your guide to building a program on solid ground. It's a simple way for you to think through how to plan, operate, and evaluate your B2B marketing campaigns and communicate their success, both within your team and across your organization. Target, engage, activate, and measure are your building blocks, and with them, you can construct a B2B skyscraper.

APPLYING TEAM TO THE B2B MATURITY CURVE

You might want to refer to Section 2 for a more detailed explanation of the B2B Maturity Curve, but here is the flashcard version: The curve allows organizations to assess where their B2B marketing efforts fall along the path of average to good to great. You can apply the curve to your overall marketing program, or to your specific performance according to the TEAM Framework.

Let's break down what we mean by average, good, and great marketing. Hint: It's all about growth and the influence of marketing on achievement of organizational goals. Average marketing, or, for many companies, the status quo, is inefficient marketing. Growth is hindered because processes aren't in place to foster organizational alignment. Leads often are overvalued, salespeople aren't given actionable data, and the wrong metrics are measured.

In terms of TEAM, we can define average marketing more succinctly:

Targeting: disconnected

Engagement: quantity

Activation: reactive

Measurement: funnel

With a few account-based techniques applied, organizations can take their B2B marketing from average to good quickly. They won't be crushing it at full scale, but they might experience efficient growth within the smaller programs they're running. That's good, because your B2B evolution should start small, but this is the point on the curve where the two worlds of account-based and traditional funnel-based marketing still swirl together in a murky soup.

Lead quantity is no longer put on a pedestal, and engagement tactics are becoming more personalized for the small number of accounts marketing goes after. Sales teams still need volume to reach their numbers, however, and account-based sprints and pilot programs don't quite cut it. That means two funnels are used for measurement: one based on traditional metrics, and one tracking engagement within a certain set of accounts. Organizations that find themselves here are likely to be aligned on what their goals are, but not equipped with the tools to support them fully at scale.

As TEAM would describe it:

Targeting: static

Engagement: quality

Activation: proactive

Measurement: double funnel

Making the leap to efficient growth at scale is the holy grail for marketers. This is what full B2B maturity looks like. Marketing is aligned not only with sales and customer success in terms of goals, but also with the ability to provide full support with dynamic insights that allow for more personalized communication. Sales teams don't have to make up for lost lead volume, because quality demand is now predictable and they're able to focus on a smaller number of accounts than ever before.

At B2B 2.0, accounts are constantly moving up and down in priority based on real-time engagement insights provided by marketing. This allows #OneTeam to develop more creative solutions and provide one-to-one experiences (not just communication) that resonate with customers and turn them into advocates. Old measurement funnels go out the window here, replaced with one B2B scorecard that measures the success of the program according to metrics that matter to each unique organization.

TEAM at 2.0 looks like this:

Targeting: dynamic

Engagement: experiential

Activation: prioritized

Measurement: one scorecard

Here's the B2B Maturity Curve you can use to assess where you are on your journey, from status quo to good to great!

B2B MATURITY CURVE WITH TEAM

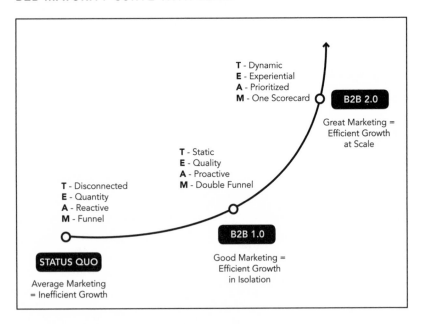

Now here's the question only you can answer:

Where do you fall on the B2B Maturity Curve?

ABM *is* **B2B.**

If you assessed yourself in the earlier section, you might now want to take another look with the fresh perspective of the TEAM Framework. Your journey to B2B 2.0 is unique to your organization, and probably won't follow a nice, clean path with all aspects of TEAM leveling up at the same time. You should have a good idea of where your targeting, activation, engagement, and measurement efforts stand on this chart. Refer back to the TEAM section when you need the most help to get everything working dynamically at scale.

Here's another way to visualize the curve in terms of TEAM. It includes your tech stack, sales, and marketing relationship as well as the organizational readiness that correspond to the outcomes of your unique business model:

B2B MATURITY FRAMEWORK

Status Quo (where you've been)	B2B 1.0 (where you might be)	B2B 2.0 (where you are going)
Disconnected: Leads at all cost	**Static**: Pilot program "Top 100 list"	**Dynamic**: Run you biz at scale "Always on"
Quantity	**Quality**	**Experiential**
Reactive sales alerts	**Proactive** sales alerts	**Prioritized** sales alerts
Funnel	Double Funnel	One Scorecard
CRM + MA	7000+ shiny new objects — best of breed	TEAM-based tech stack — smaller and tightly integrated
Sales-driven or Marketing-driven	Marketing + Sales Alignment	Sales + Marketing + CS acting as #OneTeam
Inefficient growth	Efficient **growth** model **in isolation**	**Efficient growth model at scale**

You can see how this blueprint might be applied to the B2B home you're building, but you still need the right tools to hammer and plaster your way to more revenue. The TEAM Framework is designed to be prescriptive and actionable as you go from average to good to great in all aspects of marketing, and that includes your tech stack. Let's walk through how TEAM can help you make sense of your technology so you can stop chasing the tech trends and start cutting down to the tools that deliver real B2B results.

How to Build a TEAM-based Tech Stack

More than 8,000 pieces of marketing technology are on the market now. How do you know which ones to choose for your tech stack? If you're like most organizations, you've made a habit of chasing the latest and greatest tools developed every year, hoping that you'll find the perfect new piece to bring all of your programs together. The reality is that without a strategic approach aligned with running your business more efficiently at scale, each new piece of marketing technology only adds to your mounting frustrations.

As a marketer, you should be able to approach your CEO or CFO and have a real business conversation about technology.

As a marketer, you should be able to approach your CEO or CFO and have a real business conversation about technology. We've seen successful companies greatly reduce the number of tools in their tech stack simply by applying TEAM Framework thinking. You don't want another shiny new toy; you want something that will help your business grow. The most efficient way to achieve growth at scale is to target, engage, activate sales, and measure better.

Few companies have a strategic reason for structuring their tech stacks the way they do. By looking for tools designed to help you specifically across the TEAM Framework, you'll be able to fit together tools that work with each other to achieve the same business outcomes. Your goal should be to trim your toolkit to exactly the options you need to target, engage, activate, and measure. We've included some of our favorite, best-of-breed tools in each category as of May 1, 2019.

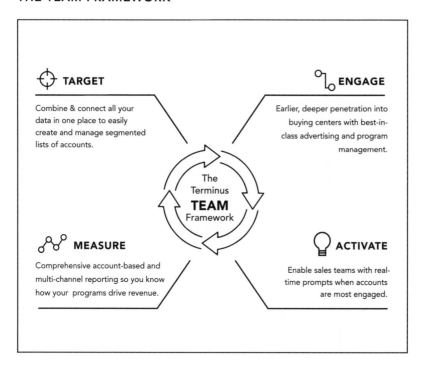

How to Operationalize TEAM across the Account Life Cycle

B2B marketing encompasses the entire customer life cycle, from advance targeting of select accounts to renewal of longtime customers. Every life cycle includes seven core growth strategies, organized into three stages: acquisition, acceleration, and expansion. The TEAM Framework helps to unify these strategies so they all work in tandem, informing one another and developing a dynamic, always-on B2B program to reach goals that are unique to your organization.

Just to refresh your memory, here are the basic strategies at play during each stage:

Acquisition: top-of-the-funnel demand generation
KPIs: website and marketing engagement

Acceleration: Moving pipeline through each stage of the sales process.
KPIs: velocity between stages

Expansion: Revenue focus within current customer base by increasing contract size, introducing new products, and retaining current customers.
KPIs: TCV, pipeline, revenue, and retention rates

This B2B marketing playbook demonstrates how the TEAM Framework can be applied to influence growth throughout the life cycle.

ABM PLAYBOOK

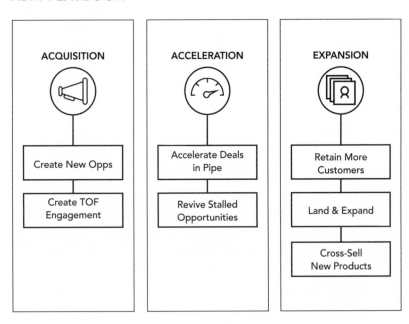

Depending on where you identify yourself on the B2B Maturity Curve, you should have a good idea of the types of programs that would be most beneficial to run and the stages and strategies you could improve upon to move your organization toward B2B 2.0.

On the following pages, you'll find sample worksheets for your pleasure in ripping out, copying, and writing on. These worksheets will get you and your team thinking about your program goals, the key stakeholders within your organization, and specific ways you can target, engage, activate, and measure to achieve success.

Let's walk through examples of three types of programs you might run. We have filled out the acquisition worksheets for you as a starting point, showing the level of detail you should strive for when applying the TEAM Framework to your program.

ACQUISITION PROGRAM

Acquisition is typically defined as top-of-the-funnel demand generation.

Common acquisition program goals:

Pre-targeting: Generating awareness with businesses that are not familiar with the organization.

Engagement and nurture: Creating interest within buying centers that have not entered the sales process.

Key stakeholders: Demand generation, digital marketing, marketing operations, and sales development.

Common acceleration program goals:

Acceleration is typically defined as moving pipeline through each stage of the sales process.

Pipeline acceleration: Coordinating between marketing and sales to create and maintain momentum during the buying cycle.

Winbacks: Regenerating interest within an account where buying momentum has been lost.

Key stakeholders: Demand generation, field marketing, marketing operations, and account executives.

Common expansion program goals:

Expansion is typically defined as revenue focus within the current customer base by increasing contract size, introducing new products, and retaining current customers.

Customer retention: Maintaining revenue within existing customer accounts through regular engagement.

Cross-sell and upsell: Introducing additional products or offerings to existing buying centers in client accounts.

Land and expand: Introducing products and offerings to new buying centers within existing client accounts.

Key stakeholders: Customer marketing, marketing operations, customer success, and account executives

Sample acquisition program worksheets that walk through the entire TEAM Framework.

PART 1: PROGRAM OVERVIEW

What is the overarching Goal of the Program?
Acquisition

Program Name
Boston Area Software Product Demand Generation

Describe the Program
Drive demand generation in the Northeast region for Software Product. Focus on enterprise accounts in the high tech and manufacturing industries to create awareness, and drive new business pipeline opportunities for the account executives. We will use a multi-threaded approach across cross functional team members.

Desired Outcomes
Generate new business opportunities in the Northeast region

ABM *is* **B2B.**

Key Internal Stakeholders
Director of Demand Generation, Head of Northeast Sales, C-suite executives

Primary Program Manager
Nancy Jones, Director Demand Gen

Overall Program Budget
$50,000

Length of Program
One quarter

Platforms Leveraged
Terminus, Sendoso/PFL, Salesloft, Salesforce, Marketo

Define the Control Group
We'll use the Northeast program to pilot a comprehensive account based outreach, we'll compare the success of the program against accounts of the same profile that are outside of the Northeast region and not receiving any account based outreach.

Identify Accounts or Efforts that are not in Scope
All efforts for this program are specific to creating new opportunities within good fit prospect accounts in the Northeast for our Software Product. Other product line promotion or accounts in other regions are not in scope.

Other Notes
Based on our success in this program, we can leverage our learnings to scale and launch additional regional programs to promote our Software Product.

PART 2: TARGET

Which accounts will you Target?
Good fit accounts in the Greater Boston Area with Marketing Responses but no open opportunities.

Which team members are involved in determining accounts in the list?
Marketing Operations for insights into the appropriate data fields. Sales for alignment.

What attributes will narrow the list of potential accounts to define the identified accounts for this program?
High Tech & Manufacturing Industry, Employee Size over 500, Revenue Range over $1M, Northeast Region, Fit Score of 80+

What data sources will you leverage?
Firmographic data, Salesforce account data

How often will you update the accounts on the list?
Quarterly

Who is responsible for managing updates to the list as needed?
Shirley, Marketing Operations Manager

Other Notes
None

ABM *is* B2B.

PART 3: ENGAGE

What strategies will you leverage to Engage the identified accounts?
Account-based advertising, Direct mail, ADR outbound, Industry happy hour meet-ups

What is the messaging for the outreach?
Top minds in Boston use our software

Which assets will be leveraged?
Landing page for event registration
CEO invite to C-suite (DM)
Gartner Report on software
Local Boston company case study

Which team members are involved?
Shirley, Marketing Operations Manager
Donna, Digital Manager
George, ADR Manager
Freddie, Northeast Field Marketing Manager

What platforms will be leveraged?
Terminus, Sendoso, Marketo, Salesloft

Who is responsible for orchestration?
Freddie Field Marketing - Event Management
Donna Digital - Ad Creative, Terminus Campaign
George - ADR Outreach

Other Notes
Use Terminus Campaign Analytics to identify successful content/messaging and event types for the Northeast region based on regional closed won opportunities.

PART 4: ACTIVATE

Define the process for disseminating Terminus platform data to Activate members of your Sales teams.
Create Salesforce Engagement Spike report for Northeast ADRs to prioritize outreach leading up to events. Create an account list filtered by account owner to allow ADRs to see what marketing messaging accounts are engaging with. Train the ADR team about the reports and resources available.

Which key data points will sales teams retrieve or receive?
Ad impressions/Clicks from account list, Page views from account list, Engagement spike notifications, Event registrations, Other campaign responses from accounts on account list.

What is the cadence for attaining data?
Spike notifications are delivered automatically on a weekly basis. Other campaign information will be updated in real time.

What is the desired sales action?
Reps should bookmark the account list in the hub to continuously keep track of new marketing activity and reach out with designated messaging. Use the weekly spike report to prioritize outreach based on engaged accounts.

Who is responsible for ensuring sales is receiving the necessary information?
Shirley, Marketing Operations Manager

Who is responsible for attaining buy-in from sales leadership?
George, ADR Manager & Caroline, CMO

Which team members are involved?
ADR Team, Marketing Ops, Demand Gen for program oversight

PART 5: MEASURE

What tools will be used to Measure success of the overall program?
Terminus Scorecard, Terminus Campaign Analytics, Salesloft reports, Google Analytics

Which KPIs will be used to determine the success of the overall program?
# of Opportunities/$ Pipeline created # of Event attendees

# of Campaign Responses within account list # of Deals/$ Revenue closed

How often will these be measured?
# of Campaign Responses - Weekly
# of Opps/Pipeline - Weekly
# of Event attendees - After each event
# of Deals/$ Revenue - Quarterly

Which team members are involved in measurement?
Marketing Operations to manage the reporting, full team responsible for reviewing data and iterating

When will results be reported to the greater team? Monthly

Other Notes

Leverage the reporting regularly, not just monthly to track leading indicators. Use the directional data to tweak engagement programs for optimal performance.

Additional worksheets for acquisition, acceleration, and expansion strategies are available for download at terminus.com/ABMisB2B.

Download (it's free) and print these out so you can be on your way to buildingi your TEAM-based programs with clarity and purpose.

HOW TO STRUCTURE YOUR TEAM

Now that you know where your organization falls on the B2B Maturity Curve, what a TEAM-based tech stack looks like, and how the TEAM Framework can be applied to generate revenue across the entire customer life cycle, it looks as if our work here is done! Bye!

Oh, you're still wondering where that leaves your current marketing team? Of course. Every marketing department has different goals, and organizations are unique in how they structure their teams, assign job titles, and delegate responsibilities and areas of focus.

The fact that ABM, and, by extension, the TEAM Framework, touches every aspect of B2B marketing means that each employee in the marketing department could be involved with every part of executing an account-based strategy. That would be inefficient, so the question becomes: How do you decide how to best use your people? Speaking to CMOs specifically, how do you want to build your marketing team to drive revenue around the TEAM Framework? Form follows function, and team structure can tell you a lot about what's really important to the head of marketing and the company as a whole.

It's all about defining specific business goals that marketing will help your organization achieve.

It's all about defining specific business goals that marketing will help your organization achieve. With B2B, you need to look beyond job titles and think about primary responsibilities. Titles alone don't tell the whole story of what marketers actually do in B2B; two people with the same title might have wildly different day-to-day tasks, depending on the type of team they're on.

We developed a few top-level examples of marketing department structure to help you identify gaps and allocate personnel resources to solidify your team, based on TEAM. We're not advocating that you hire and fire now to get your marketing department looking exactly like these sample departments. Instead, we're suggesting

ABM *is* **B2B.**

some structures we've noted as effective when built around the areas of focus a marketing leader cares about most.

Let's look at a few common ways to organize your marketing team with the TEAM Framework in mind. Within each structure, you'll see:

- Who is involved, with job title
- Individual KPIs to focus on
- Elements of TEAM

FOCUS: FUNCTIONAL BALANCE

FOCUSED ON FUNCTIONAL BALANCE

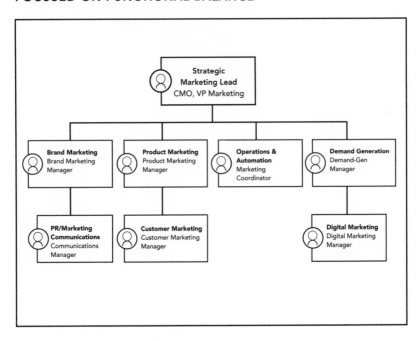

This is probably the most common example of a marketing organization structure, and it's even more common the smaller the team is. The main focus is collaborating and creating alignment across content, messaging, automation, and demand gen. With functional balance, there are no gaps even when one person is out; there's always someone to slide right in and pick up the slack.

ABM *is* **B2B.**

FOCUSED ON FUNCTIONAL BALANCE: KPIs

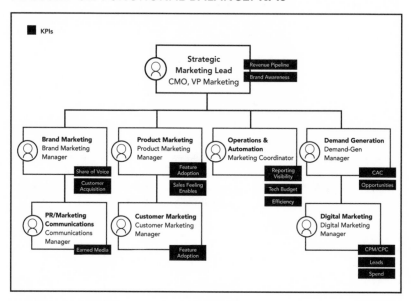

Because this type of team is so lean and well-versed in many aspects of marketing, there's probably some cross-pollination with responsibilities. In this example, brand, product, and customer marketing all are involved in content creation, and communications shares email campaign duties with operations.

FOCUSED ON FUNCTIONAL BALANCE: **TEAM**

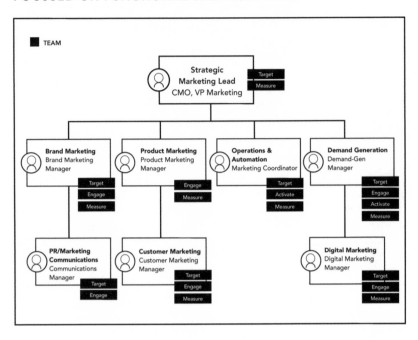

Employees in a functional balance structure have slightly broader job responsibilities, with operations/automation being the biggest jack-of-all-trades. Functions executed by the marketing coordinator include email building, project managing, reporting, and supporting digital media.

FOCUS: DRIVING THROUGH THE FUNNEL

FOCUSED ON DRIVING THROUGH THE FUNNEL

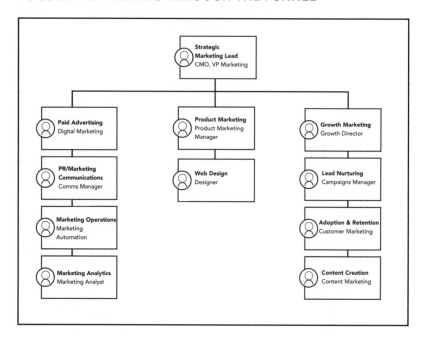

This structure is popular within organizations that are high-performing and lead-based. That's why there's an entire arm dedicated to growth as well as a team that's focused on lead-nurturing through content creation, campaigns, and automation further down the funnel.

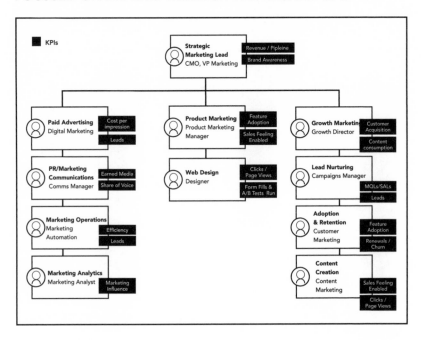

Within this structure, there's a separate top-of-funnel team comprising digital, branding/PR and its own automation person. At the center is a product-marketing team that supports messaging developed by both sides.

FOCUSED ON DRIVING THROUGH THE FUNNEL: **TEAM**

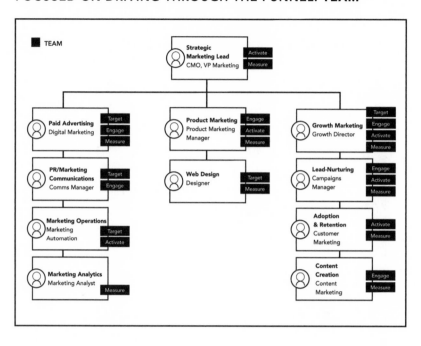

FOCUS: DISTRIBUTED FIELD MARKETING WITHIN LINES OF BUSINESS

DISTRIBUTED FIELD MARKETING WITHIN LINES OF BUSINESS

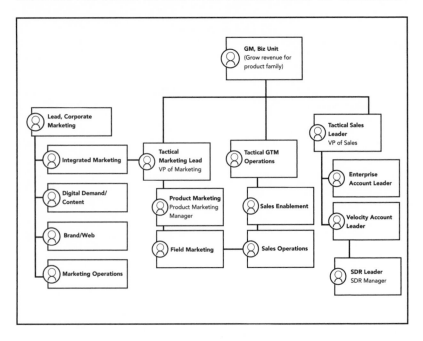

This is a structure suited for larger enterprises in which teams are segmented by product line or region. We're talking international business, helmed by the GM of a particular unit focused on revenue growth for a specific product family. You'll also notice that sales/SDRs and marketing are aligned under the same umbrella.

Corporate marketing, with broad comms, overall value prop, social strategy, and corporate analytics, is segmented from business unit teams with product marketing, sales enablement, and field and event marketing. In this example, the corporate marketing team is a single team, and the business unit teams scale based on need for products, regions, etc. The corporate team also usually falls under a different leadership structure.

ABM *is* **B2B.**

FOCUS: MARKETING AND SALES ALIGNMENT

FOCUSED ON MARKETING AND SALES ALIGNMENT

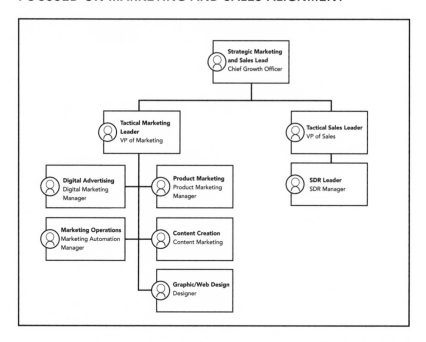

If there's one thing we hope is clear by now, it's that marketing and sales alignment are imperative to running a successful ABM program. A marketing structure with alignment as the main focus is a great way to set yourself up for the requirements of ABM.

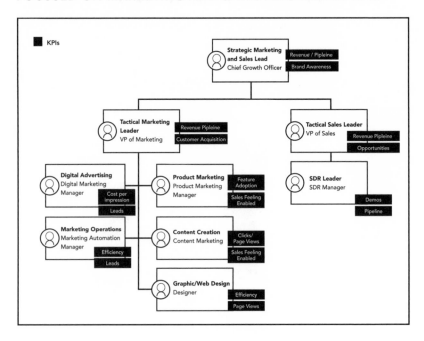

This particular example is more appropriate for mid-market and smaller organizations. It gives strategic leaders immediate insight into metrics because they're so nicely aligned. There's no more measuring of marketing on leads or sales on opportunities and revenue.

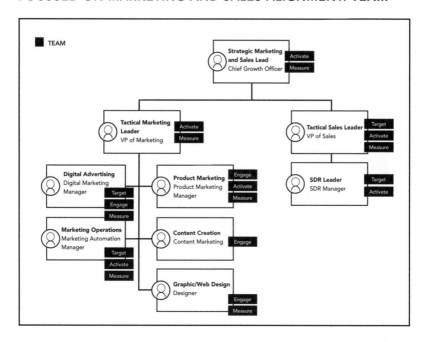

This type of functional alignment is all about driving business growth, so the leader is listed as the chief growth officer, not the chief marketing officer. There's also less focus on driving demand with current customers; hence the omission of customer marketing in this example. For smaller organizations, product marketing and content marketing could be done by the same person; likewise with a digital advertising person and designer.

Now you should have everything you need to start making your TEAM dreams a reality. This framework gives you a consistent model around which to structure your organization, technology, and programs. It becomes the one simple check against which all your efforts can be scrutinized: Is what I'm doing helping me to more effectively target, engage, activate, or measure across the customer life cycle? If not, it has no place in your organization. If it is, you're on track for a business transformation driven by marketing on a scale you've never experienced before.

Pro tip: You can download all these resources on terminus.com/ABMisB2B.

The TEAM framework

- How to build an ABM stack
- The state of ABM
- Seven strategies to get started with ABM
- TEAM workbook for acquisition strategy
- TEAM workbook for acceleration strategy
- TEAM workbook for expansion strategy
- How to assess where you are on the TEAM-based B2B Maturity Curve
- TEAM-based LinkedIn course on ABM foundations

Want to learn and grow as a team?

Go to the LinkedIn course on account-based marketing foundations. It's a one-hour course jam-packed with 19 videos that outline the TEAM Framework and many other concepts from this book. You can get your team together for lunch, order some pizza, take the course, and become officially LinkedIn ABM-certified.

How cool is that?

Finally, remember that we are using ABM and B2B interchangeably because we believe, and hope by now that you do, too: ABM is B2B.

Go ahead and tweet this up: #ABMisB2B

Go ahead and tweet this up: #ABMisB2B

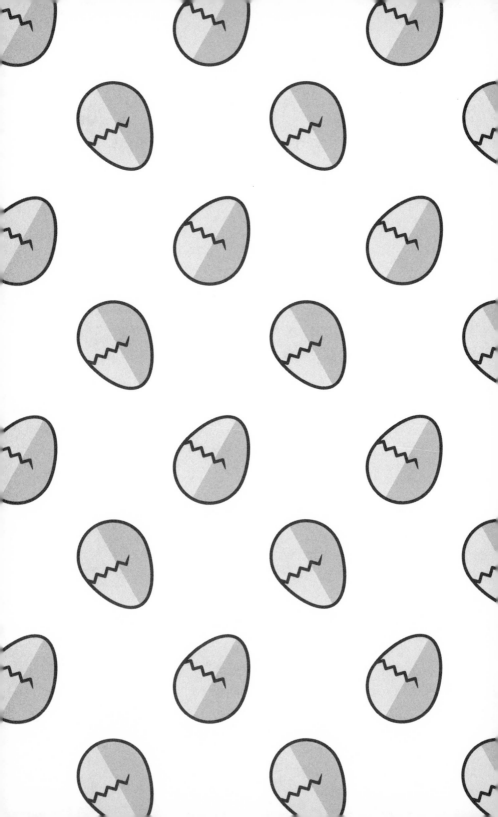

SECTION 5

FROM BORING TO BORING

to Bonus 2 Bonus

THE TOP PEOPLE, AUTHORS, AND PODCAST EPISODES TO FOLLOW ON YOUR PATH TO B2B TRANSFORMATION

If you have read until here, you are our hero, and now we want to introduce you to other heroes. No organization transforms alone. We certainly didn't, and we owe much of our success to customers and peers who have shown us what's possible with B2B marketing. Whenever we see an amazing application of account-centric thinking or read a mind-blowing metric from someone in our industry, we get so excited, we have to pick their brain and discover how they did it. That's how the FlipMyFunnel community was born: from curiosity in ourselves combined with the genius of others.

If this book has changed the way you think about marketing, we can assure you, it's only the tip of the iceberg. We're always learning and improving thanks to our friends and colleagues, and we want to open up our network to you.

Enjoy our ever-growing list of content from brilliant people who can help you achieve Business to Business mega-success.

TOP 24 EPISODES OF THE FLIPMYFUNNEL PODCAST ON B2B TRANSFORMATION

The FlipMyFunnel daily podcast, which is now in the top 50 business podcast on iTunes with over 500 five star reviews (humble brag), is pure B2B gold wrapped in a neat, half-hour package. These are some of our favorite episodes, featuring business leaders talking about B2B marketing, sales, and leadership lessons that will help you transform your business.

EPISODE 331

MICHAEL ROSE

CEO, Founder, Mojo Media Labs. Author, *ROE Powers ROI*

TOPIC

Running an agency with your wife and crushing it

KEY TAKEAWAYS

Great cultures will get you through bad times. Change is hard, andgreat teams see change as an opportunity.

Transparency is the key to establishing the foundation of a great TEAM.

EPISODE 297

HEIDI MELIN

CMO, Workfront

TOPIC

How to make a difference at work and in your career

KEY TAKEAWAYS

It's not who you know, it's how you treat them.

Listen to your gut.

Know when to say, "Enough!"

EPISODE 292

RUTH ROWANN
Global CMO, Dimension Data

TOPIC

How a leader brings about change and gets everyone on board

KEY TAKEAWAYS

Your "why" is the most important thing you need to clarify for your team. Without it, you have no chance of getting buy-in.

Resistance comes when you don't take the time to explain this to your team or engage them in taking ownership of their role in shaping the future. A team of smart people can do amazing things.

Change is constant.

EPISODE 287

GENE FOCA
CMO, Getty Images

TOPIC

Creating a frictionless customer experience

KEY TAKEAWAYS

The best teams are not necessarily made up of A-players.

Everyone on your team is responsible for creating a customer journey that is frictionless.

Every person on the executive team is responsible for the company's brand.

EPISODE 282

JENNIFER DIMAS
CMO: EGNYTE

TOPIC

Six success secrets of a CMO

KEY TAKEAWAYS

How do you know when you're ready to make the leap to CMO? Ask your peers.

Use your first weeks with the company to learn about everything but marketing. You'll need to observe how all the parts work together so you can understand what and how the company delivers to its customers.

As a new CMO, you will probably inherit a team rather than get the chance to create one from scratch.

Start by investigating the roles that need to be filled rather than their job titles. You may find that everyone is shouldering a task that should be done by a dedicated person or team.

EPISODE 261

CORINNE SKYLAR
CMO: IBM iX

TOPIC

How to build world-class teams

KEY TAKEAWAYS

Humans and people are at the center of all businesses.

You can have the greatest ideas in the world, but if you're not able to execute on those ideas and don't have the experience to really bring those ideas to life, you're not going to go very far.

Make sure you have alignment throughout your entire organization.

EPISODE 250

JEN GRANT
CMO: Looker

TOPIC

What are the top priorities of a #CMO who just happened to raise
$103 million with $1.6 billion in valuation?

KEY TAKEAWAYS

"We need to actually write it down. We need to capture it. Because if we don't,
you're going to hire a bunch of executives and be a thousand-person company,
and nobody will say what [the culture] is."

Elevate your customer experience to encompass the entire customer journey.
Marketing efforts and superb customer experiences don't end when a client signs
up for your product or service; that's when the real work begins!

In order for ABM to be implemented, it requires sales reps to buy in and be
involved with marketing efforts.

EPISODE 231

KAREN STEELE
CMO: LeanData

TOPIC

3 ways to challenge your marketing team to drive the only metric that matters

KEY TAKEAWAYS

Everyone owns revenue. Revenue doesn't fall under the CRO. It isn't owned by
sales.

As marketers, we have to partner with sales in order to create a #OneTeam effort
that drives all efforts toward a common goal. The silos of organizations have to be

destroyed in order to communicate and rally around the only metric that matters: revenue growth.

Is accurate data flowing through your team? Routing leads, matching the right accounts, having shared metrics, etc. … Whatever your plan is, here's the bottom line: When it comes to expediting your revenue process, there has to be a plan to get the right data to the right person at the right time.

EPISODE 225

KIRBY WADSWORTH
CMO: Illusive Networks

TOPIC
How a four-time CMO says you should create your ideal customer profile.

KEY TAKEAWAYS
ABM is easy as soon as soon as you define your original ideal customer profile.

"These characteristics don't necessarily make sense in the beginning when we're looking at the data; it's later that they start to bubble up, and you see that they do make sense."

"The first thing is to tier your existing funnel, based on your ICP characteristics; then you have to reformulate your entire go-to market to ensure you're targeting customers who meet that ICP criteria."

EPISODE 210

KYLE LACY
VP, Marketing, Lessonly

TOPIC
What it takes to be a modern CMO

KEY TAKEAWAYS

Be flexible as your company grows. The role of a modern CMO or marketing leader requires an incredible array of unique functions, competencies, and skills. Further, you must have a high degree of emotional intelligence to interact with various people, within your department and outside of it, to accomplish all this. There is an incredible amount of left and right brain intellect.

"You have to be obsessed with the entire customer journey from prospect to upsell."

Because of the evolution of the role, the essential funding mentality must also shift: At some point in your growth, you have to be okay with spending money on results that are difficult to measure. You will have to invest in brand.

EPISODE 210

JUSTIN KELLER
VP, Marketing- Sigstr

TOPIC

What it takes to be a modern CMO

KEY TAKEAWAYS

"The most impactful things your marketing team can do are things that are not scalable."

There is a premium on brand and on things you can't use numbers to analyze.

Determine the current state of growth of your company, and apply your skills and resources to the area that will make the most impact right now.

EPISODE 204

TIM KOPP
Former CMO, General Partner, Managing Director, Hyde Park Venture Partners (Indianapolis office)

TOPIC

How to run a board meeting as a rockstar CMO

KEY TAKEAWAYS

"Marketing exists to support sales, at the end of the day."

"You have to have command and mastery over your business at a financial level."

The board is filled with allies who want you to succeed.

EPISODE 172

ALEX GOBBI
CMO, Secureworks

TOPIC

What makes a great chief marketing officer?

KEY TAKEAWAYS

What does it look like to be a modern CMO?

It looks like knowing your brand, embracing creativity, utilizing data, having a great attitude, and empowering others.

"I love the magic that happens when you combine creativity with deep analytics, and I think marketing really allows you to do that."

Without understanding your brand, you cannot creatively portray it.

EPISODE 172

KIRA MONDRUS
SVP Global Marketing at Tricentis

TOPIC

What makes a great chief marketing officer?

ABM *is* **B2B.**

KEY TAKEAWAYS

Without brand, you cannot create demand.

"As marketers, we have to really embody the voice of the customer."

Creativity grows a company. Brand sustains it.

EPISODE **127 & 107**

CHANDAR PATTABHIRAM
CMO, Coupa Software

TOPIC

Using AI to increase effectiveness in the buyer journey

KEY TAKEAWAYS

Over 85% of B2B marketing spend is focused solely on the acquisition stage of the buyer's journey.

"If someone is staying with you longer, paying you more, and shouting from the rooftops, invariably, you're doing good as a business."

Figuring out the right time to cross-sell to existing customers will then increase the lifetime value of each customer, and show even more of marketing's effects on overall revenue generation...not just at the top of the funnel.

EPISODE **122**

ROBBY GULRI
CMO, Engage Talent and CMO, Proliant

TOPIC

Winning attributes of a top marketer

KEY TAKEAWAYS

As a CMO, you will face problems. Face them head-on.

You have to understand your position so well, you can succinctly and simply explain it in a digestible way to a child.

Lead with humility and service.

EPISODE 117

MARK STROUSE
Former CMO, Honeywell Founder and CEO of Proof Analytics

TOPIC
Transitioning from CMO to CEO

KEY TAKEAWAYS
As CEO, you will spend 90% of your day on things in which you are not an expert.

It's a CEO's job to ask and answer the right questions.

As any company grows, the leader has to stop giving ideas, take a step back, and start to ask powerful questions.

EPISODE 16

KIPP BODNAR
CMO, HubSpot

TOPIC
Insights from 10 years of inbound marketing

KEY TAKEAWAYS
Relevant, personalized emails drive 18 times more revenue than broadcast emails.

The right to connect with people on social media platforms is earned, not bought.

Real relationships with customers are formed, not faked.

EPISODE 96

JULIA STEAD
VP, Marketing, Invoca

TOPIC

ABM success: Invoca's journey from implementation to optimization

KEY TAKEAWAYS

Establish a sales and marketing work group. It's not enough for the head of marketing and the head of sales to talk about ABM and then try to pass the directives down the line to managers, reps, and SDRs. You can't do ABM effectively with siloed teams.

Prioritize your resources to make sure you are selecting the right accounts. You need to devote the right resources, both in personnel and digital tools, to get this step right. ABM won't work well if you skimp on this step.

Start small to get it right. Don't go all-in too fast. Start with a small, integrated team working on a specific goal.

EPISODE 120

MEGAN LUEDERS
Chief Marketing Officer, Zenoss

TOPIC

3 things to know about pitching ABM to your board

KEY TAKEAWAYS

Get buy-in from the entire team early.

This doesn't just mean sales. It has to include leaders in customer success and renewals.

Recognize that it's a gradual process

ABM, along with new revenue responsibilities, should be seen as a new layer on top of the traditional roles of demand gen, brand awareness, and acquisition. Communicate this to the board, as it will take them time to adjust to the new terms of ABM.

Build your own ABM scorecard.

EPISODE 232

BRITTNEY OVERSTREET
Manager of Account Marketing, Signify Health

TOPIC
5 skills every ABMer must have

KEY TAKEAWAYS
"Not all accounts are the same—often they each need a personal, detailed approach."

Marketing is here to support sales, because sales grows companies.

In addition to intel you gather from sales and marketing, research is king. You have to be a great researcher to dig deep into accounts and discover what may be engaging or interesting to them.

EPISODE 259

JILLIAN GARTNER
Director of Account Based Marketing, Thomson Reuters

TOPIC
How Thomson Reuters uses these five strategies to run its ABM program at scale

KEY TAKEAWAYS
Understand each account. How many touchpoints does this account need? Does this account require a 1-to-1 approach?

ABM *is* **B2B.**

Leverage tech to get the right people at the right time.

Remember retention by providing ongoing value for your current customers.

EPISODE 274

DANIEL DAY

Senior Director, Account-Based Marketing and Market Planning, Snowflake

TOPIC

How to become an account-based marketing rockstar

KEY TAKEAWAYS

Don't create ads or landing pages that are click-baity.

Try to be prescriptive and create an experience that's worthy of your prospective customers and adds value to their day. You're trying to drive business outcomes.

Make the ads' promises as specific as possible.

EPISODE 304

JEREMY MIDDLETON

Senior Director of Digital Marketing and Revenue Operations, Pramata

TOPIC

How to break through the noise and create awareness

KEY TAKEAWAYS

Narrowing the target also helps to narrow and sharpen the messaging. In order to get the maximum bang for the buck, Pramata tiers the total addressable market in terms of who has the highest profile.

By following who felt the most pain in the target companies, Pramata discovered quickly that the personas resided in only two departments: sales operations and finance.

Pramata started with 22 marketing technology tools that overlapped. By narrowing the target market and personas, the teams were able to toss tools that no longer were part of their mission.

EPISODE 319

DANIEL ENGLEBRETSON
Director, Integrated Marketing, Phononic

TOPIC
Customer in the office: how Phononic used Terminus to reap huge ABM success

KEY TAKEAWAYS
When a new blog was released that matched a target, it was added to the Terminus cadence. Every time this happened, content engagement would spike big time.

If you don't have a huge ad budget, you can benefit from a minimal spend and use Terminus' tracking and analytics to measure how all the campaigns are interacting with the other tactics.

Phononic had a challenge. Teams were generating too many leads for sales to pursue. Too much success is a good problem to have.

EPISODE 77

MASHA FINKELSTEIN
Growth Marketing, Chrome Enterprise Google Cloud

TOPIC
How to measure ABM success

KEY TAKEAWAYS
What really matters is, are we creating deeper relationships with the right people? If we are, we're going to create more engagement. It's not about selling your product; it's about engagement.

Look at your engagement rates within those target accounts.

ABM *is* **B2B.**

Who is actually actively engaging with you and moving beyond simple interest to action?

The more people you can get involved in the same accounts, the better off you'll be in the long run.

Don't be afraid to fail. Don't be afraid to jump in and get it done. There will be a learning curve, but you'll see growth within your accounts that you never thought possible.

TOP 33 BOOK REVIEWS/AUTHOR INTERVIEWS ON FLIPMYFUNNEL THAT WILL INSPIRE YOU TO TRANSFORM YOUR ORGANIZATION

We interviewed dozens of authors, and when we couldn't meet the authors, we reviewed their books to get insights on the topics they're most passionate about in the world of B2B marketing.

EPISODE 314

SOON YU

BOOK TITLE:

Author: *Iconic Advantage: Don't Chase the New, Innovate the Old Titles:* Former Global VP of Innovation, VF Corp.; adjunct professor, The New School's Parsons School of Design

KEY TAKEAWAYS

"It isn't always the biggest, baddest, or fastest mousetrap that gets the mice. It's the one with the stinkiest cheese."

Soon helps companies realize that they don't have to be the fastest, biggest, or best stocked in technology to be successful. But they do have to connect with their audience, and the best way to do that is through meaningful marketing.

If you're innovating in an area people are already familiar with where you have internal processes in place, it's that much easier to take something old to the next level.

EPISODE 312

DAN STEINMAN + LINCOLN MURPHY

BOOK TITLE:

Co-authors: *Customer Success: How Innovative Companies Are Reducing Churn and Growing Recurring Revenue*

Steinman's title: General Manager, Gainsight EMEA
Murphy's title: Customer Success Consultant

KEY TAKEAWAYS

If you are creating a new category, the CEO is the first evangelist. The leader must create a vision that motivates the other founders, the development team, investors, and potentially the end customers.

Not everyone needs to write a book, but if you're an evangelist, it can do a lot of the heavy lifting for you. A book establishes thought leadership in your industry. It also provides a platform for speaking engagements and press interviews.

Evangelism reveals a new way of thinking about solving the pain points of your prospects at the macro. You are talking about the solution to their problem in a way that is solution-agnostic. Your company's solution is a merely one of many good ways to embody this new way of thinking.

EPISODE 311

JAY BAER
President, Convince & Convert, keynote speaker

BOOK TITLE:
Author: six best-sellers, including *Talk Triggers*

KEY TAKEAWAYS
91% of B2B purchases are influenced by word of mouth.

Figure out what the pulse of your brand is. It's important to go back and look at how your organization operates, then consider the touchpoints and how you monitor, measure, and even think about your pulse. If you don't know what the pulse of your customer is, then you don't know the pulse of your brand.

Whatever you're doing, are you doing something that your customers don't expect? That's the only way to be differentiated in the marketplace.

EPISODE 306

DAVID BRIER
Title: Chief Gravity Defyer

BOOK TITLE:

Brand Intervention

KEY TAKEAWAYS

The art of differentiation: How are you different, what makes you different, and why is somebody going to buy from you or your competitor? Cliché's suck the life out of brands. They take you away from who you are originally, who you are authentically, and the depth of your brand.

Figure out how you're making the world smaller, because that's what your customers want. They want a faster, convenient, easier process or life.

Write down how and why your product or service is different. Now look at your top two to six competing companies. Look at their messaging. If it sounds the same as yours, you need to dig a little deeper. I challenge you to look deep enough and then cross-check it, and if your promises, if your assertions, if your declarations, if the reason why you should be chosen sound similar or identical to these other companies, you haven't found your point of difference yet.

EPISODE 237

ANDY PAUL
Title: Founder, The Sales House

BOOK TITLE:

Amp up your sales and zero-time selling

KEY TAKEAWAYS

In B2B, we have to remember: Our total addressable market is not infinite. Even for a company like Salesforce with a wide market, there is a finite number of available buyers.

Instead of focusing on just pipeline, start by driving significant value to every single customer in your pipeline. Even more granular, ensure that every single interaction with every single customer drives value.

Ask yourself: "How will this next phone call or email provide value to my customer?"

Coaching isn't about increasing additional pipeline. It's about personal development. We as leaders should be developing people. We should be listening, understanding their personal and career goals, and then pushing toward that success.

EPISODE 112

ALLEN GANNETT
Chief Strategy Officer, Skyword

BOOK TITLE:

The Creative Curve

KEY TAKEAWAYS

The four laws of the creative curve:

Consumption: Everybody tends to think of creators as constantly creating, when in reality, creators are some of the most active consumers of information out there.

Imitation: Originality is idolized, but there is truth to that notion that great artists steal. Or at least they imitate. They draw inspiration from all sorts of places, imitating past successful creatives.

Community: Since creativity is a social phenomenon, you need people to agree with what you've done and validate your creativity. Otherwise, you'll have no way of knowing that what you're doing is actually creative.

Iterations: Again, there's a myth that Mozart just sat down and wrote concertos, when in reality, he went through draft after draft after draft before getting the music just right.

EPISODE 72

STU HEINECKE
President, CartoonLink Founder, Cartoonists.org, Wall Street Journal cartoonist

BOOK TITLE:
How to Get a Meeting with Anyone

KEY TAKEAWAYS

Persistence in business is the key to success. Being persistent while remaining respectful will grant you opportunities you've only dreamt of.

The second unlikely but successful aspect of landing a big meeting is timing.

Timing of contact can be the determining factor in whether or not you will get a reply or be overlooked. Phone calls and emails are two of the most common ways we reach out to those we desire to connect with in our technology-driven society.

The thing about marketing is that it's directed at people. And people love humor. If something makes you laugh, it captures your attention, and if it captures your attention, you'll want to know more. Remember that whoever you want to get a meeting with is just a person, too, and probably loves a good laugh.

EPISODE 316

SETH GODIN
Podcaster, speaker

BOOK TITLE:

This Is Marketing

KEY TAKEAWAYS

Stand for something. If you're a marketer, or you're a leader in a company, the best thing you could do is stand for something.

The role of marketing is to make change happen. There's a lot of emotion to that, because if you can move people to take action and do things, you actually have a ton of responsibility, and we should take that seriously.

Most people think a marketer's job is to spread the word. You need to tell a good story, but also converse with the audience by being the person who listens and understands.

EPISODE 2

DAVID CANCEL
Founder, Chairman, and CEO, Drift.com

BOOK TITLE:

Conversation Marketing

KEY TAKEAWAYS

One-time success in business means nothing. To really make it, you've got to learn how to find that same amazing result again and again.

So what sets successful companies apart for others? The pursuit of progression. We have the ability to create our own reality rather than have our reality created for us. One mentality is that life and business happen to you, and the other is that you create them.

Simply stated: "If it doesn't feel right, it isn't right." The universe has given us an internal compass, and we should use it. Our spidey senses come naturally to us, but we allow a lot of other stuff to cloud that intuition.

EPISODE 66

KEENAN
CEO/President and Chief Antagonist at A Sales Guy

BOOK TITLE:

Gap Selling

KEY TAKEAWAYS

At the heart of ABM is content.

Taking the time to understand your customers' processes provides you with the knowledge to then modify and reshape, not only to enhance the impact of your service to them, but also to increase their profits.

Customers are looking to you to be the industry experts. If that image is not evoked in their minds, they are not going to take action on what you say. An effective ABM strategy calls for you to create this persona via a knowledge gap.

EPISODE 286

CLAY SCROGGINS
Lead Pastor, North Point Community Church

BOOK TITLE:

How to Lead When You Are Not in Charge

KEY TAKEAWAYS

You don't need to wait until that promotion to start being a leader. Lead right where you are. A job title and/or a higher position doesn't create a leader.

Leadership is not about authority, your position, or your title. It's about influence. Influence has to be cultivated. And guess what? You can grow influence.

How do you start leading? By leading yourself.

EPISODE 307

GUY KAWASAKI
Marketing Specialist, Venture Capitalist

BOOK TITLE:

Wise Guy

KEY TAKEAWAYS

Evangelism is the purest form of sales.

Look for tough experiences in life to grow.

Focus on improving people's lives.

EPISODE 227

MARCUS SHERIDIAN
President, Marcus Sheridan International, andPartner IMPACT

BOOK TITLE:

They Ask, You Answer

KEY TAKEAWAYS

We spend so much time trying to impress our audience that our intended message suffers. We don't try to understand how our audience speaks, how they talk, or how they understand—we are far too interested in sounding intelligent. Stop impressing your audience, and start communicating in a way they understand.

Be the game-changer that leads your industry with disclosure, and watch competitors play catch-up.

"Marketers struggle to get buy-in because they speak like marketers, and they don't speak like the business owner."

ABM *is* **B2B.**

EPISODE **73**

DANIEL PINK

BOOK TITLE:

Drive, When, and To Sell Is Human

KEY TAKEAWAYS

Keep the customer in the room. Amazon's Jeff Bezos has an empty chair in his office and in his meetings every single time. Why?

The empty chair represents the customer. This is a significant way of showing that he, along with his team, is always going to have the customer in the room.

Talking about a future customer as a future customer rather than a prospect humanizes them in a way. They're not the object of a deal you're trying to close.

Pink says to think about these three things: Seek great information. Sense what's really happening. Share back to them exactly what you have heard.

EPISODE **288**

MARC BENIOFF
Founder, Chairman, and Co-CEO, Salesforce

BOOK TITLE:

Behind the Cloud

KEY TAKEAWAYS

Focus on the 20% that makes 80% of the difference.

"The business of business is improving the state of the world."

Identify the obstacles you might hit along the way to achieving your vision. Then think about how to address them.

EPISODE 248

ANDY STANLEY
Senior Pastor, North Point Community Church; founder, North Point Ministries

BOOK TITLE:
Communicating for a Change

KEY TAKEAWAYS

Don't start with the problem. Too many organizations state the issue, then expect automatic buy-in. People aren't made that way. They don't buy into problems; they buy into people.

Speak to each individual.

You have their attention. Go straight to the solution.

EPISODE 93

DONALD MILLER
CEO, StoryBrand; workshop teacher

KEY TAKEAWAYS

All great movies have a few things in common: There's a main character who encounters a problem, meets a guide, gets helped along the way from that guide, and then defeats the bad guys.

That story plays an enormous role in the B2B world. It drives our purpose and defines why we do what we do. It gives us our why.

What we do as a business is create a space for problems to be solved. We enable the hero to save the day, and at the end of the day, to be recognized for the hero he or she is.

EPISODE 203

JEREMY DONOVAN
Group Vice President of Marketing, Gartner

BOOK TITLE:

How to Deliver a TED Talk

KEY TAKEAWAYS

The personal story: This opening works well for any speaker. Even Steve Jobs and other globally known speakers open with a story to create a personal connection with their listeners. As a way to get people's attention, a real-life story of what happened to you can't be topped.

Shocking statement: Another way to arrest people's attention is through a shocking statement. Start with "Did you know...?" For example, in a talk on the world water crisis, ask, "Did you know that one billion people lack access to a secure supply of clean water?" Use this approach if you don't have a relevant personal story.

The very important question: Ask a very important question that will get people thinking. For instance, "In B2B, the value of marketing is defined by what?" This approach makes everybody lean in to answer the question.

EPISODE 188

HAL ELROD
Keynote Speaker

BOOK TITLE:

Miracle Morning

KEY TAKEAWAYS

We live in a culture of noise, so silence is difficult. It's uncomfortable. Being alone with your thoughts can be hard.

Whether it's prayer, meditation, breathing, or whatever it looks like for you, you get quiet, you block out chatter, and you start your day by being calm.

If you don't believe in yourself, nobody else will. So affirmations or words of encouragement are vital. Say things, good things, out loud about yourself.

Much like affirmations, visualization is where you picture yourself accomplishing the things you want to accomplish.

EPISODE 98

AL RIES AND JACK TROUT
Co-founder and Chairman, Ries & Ries, Founder and Owner, Trout & Partners

BOOK TITLE:
The 22 Immutable Laws of Marketing

KEY TAKEAWAYS

Whoever is the leader in a category defines the category. The leader has a nearly unfair advantage over all other competitors. As the leader, he or she is the first in people's hearts and minds.

If you aren't the leader in your category, create a new one.

In marketing's battle, the battle of perception, people have limited mental resources. They can't remember every message, every mantra, and every value of your company. But you know what people do remember? One word.

EPISODE 258-263-268 -273

JEFF BEZOS
Founder, Chairman, CEO, and President, Amazon

BOOK TITLE:

Shareholder letter series

KEY TAKEAWAYS

To grow long-term, market leadership is the first measure of success.

Brand is a key pillar of success. Brand can feel elusive, but often your brand comes down to customer obsession.

Invent boldly.

EPISODE 83

PETER DRUCKER
Management consultant, educator

BOOK TITLE:

The Effective Executive

KEY TAKEAWAYS

What needs to be done? This sounds simple. But how many times a day do we stop and ask ourselves, "What needs to be done?"

If you determine what is right for the company, it will end up being what is right for the team and for the individual.

Develop an action plan. Don't simply ask yourself the right questions, then stop after you have the answers. Develop actionable steps to accomplishing those goals.

EPISODE 242

JOEY COLEMAN
Chief Experience Composer, Design Symphony

BOOK TITLE:

Never Lose a Customer Again

KEY TAKEAWAYS

Customer experience is about how the customer feels toward you.

Don't just sell a product, perform for your audience.

"Customer service is what you do when the customer has a problem. Customer experience is all the interactions that create how the customer feels about you."

EPISODE 28

ROBIN SHARMA
Leadership/personal mastery speaker

BOOK TITLE:

The Monk Who Sold His Ferrari

KEY TAKEAWAYS

The Monk Who Sold His Ferrari makes me take a good look at myself and what I choose to value. It makes me ask of myself and those around me, "Are we running too hard and killing ourselves? Or are we running with a passion and a purpose?"

There's nothing wrong with running our races well. Let's make sure we're running for the right reasons.

EPISODE 256

RAND FISHKIN
CEO and co-founder, SparkToro and SEOmoz

BOOK TITLE:

Lost and Founder

KEY TAKEAWAYS

Without a community, you are a commodity.

Marketers can have strong manipulative tendencies. A big part of the nature of being a marketer is figuring out how something works so you can use it to bring your message to the top.

Marketers need to discover all the places, publications, and people that their audience pays attention to, then do marketing in those places.

EPISODE 142

DAVID LEWIS
CEO, Demand Gen; speaker, podcaster

BOOK TITLE:

Manufacturing Demand

KEY TAKEAWAYS

There's something special hidden in the word *you* that changes when you're presenting. It makes your brain perk up and listen.

You must have strong openings and closes.

Cast your vision with visuals.

EPISODE 284

TRISH BERTUZZI
Founder and CEO, The Bridge Group

BOOK TITLE:

The Sales Development Playbook

KEY TAKEAWAYS

Math matters.

All these accounts have different amounts of spend and energy that need to be applied to them. The most important thing you can do is figure out exactly who you want to target, so you are not wasting your money on accounts that don't need an expensive effort.

One size does not fit all. Taking your same strategies and utilizing them for all the market types won't cut it. A mid-market account win is simple; your goal is to rise above the white noise to stand out with customers.

Campaigns matter. We have to do things differently. No longer can you spam your way into an account. Messaging matters, and as you continue up the food chain, what you say makes a huge difference.

EPISODE 197

DAVID MEERMAN SCOTT
Online marketing strategist, entrepreneur, bestselling author of 10 books

BOOK TITLE:

The New Rules of Marketing and PR

KEY TAKEAWAYS

Newsjacking is a simple idea. You take breaking news, and you jack it—you take what's going on, in real time, and you produce content that ties the frenzied story to your product and business.

"Newsjacking is the art and science of injecting your ideas into a breaking news story to generate attention, media hits, and sales."

Google indexes blogs and videos in real time. If you're agile and move rapidly, the media may pick you up, as they're looking for outsider input for their stories.

Further, many are looking to buy a product or service pertaining to a news story, so be ready to capitalize.

EPISODE 152

TODD CAPONI
Principal and Founder, Sales Melon; keynote speaker

BOOK TITLE:
The Transparency Sale

KEY TAKEAWAYS
"The brain, if it feels like it's being sold to, will put up barriers."

Your vulnerabilities are not a laundry list of all the things you're terrible at. They are an authentic representation of where you've chosen to spend less attention in an effort to make something else great.

By approaching your buyers from a place of authenticity, you're going to see that customer relationship build much more quickly, you're going to win more deals, and you're going to qualify deals out faster.

EPISODE 196

JOSEPH JAFFE
Founder and CEO, Evol8tion, author, podcaster

BOOK TITLE:
Flip the Funnel

KEY TAKEAWAYS

Your existing customers have the potential to be your best advocates. When customers of yours have an exceptional experience, they are going to tell others about it. They might even give you ideas on how to improve your business. But this starts to happen only when you think of retention from the customer point of view, not in terms of what you can get from them in return.

Acknowledgement: Make sure you take the time to say thank you to your customers.

Incentivization: Recognize and reward your customers for their loyalty and support.

EPISODE 32

MARK ORGAN
Founder and CEO of Influitive

BOOK TITLE:
The Message Is the Messenger

KEY TAKEAWAYS

We are all human, and in business, customers can relate to stories that are authentic.

Authenticity builds momentum, naturally causing people to talk about your product or your company. This is advocate marketing. The future of successful organizations lies in harnessing the power of advocate marketing. To be able to market through trusted associates, advocates, or affiliates tells the market that we don't have to tell you our product is great; our users will do it for us. It's genuine, and they systematically do it every single time.

TOP 25 B2B INFLUENCERS TO FOLLOW

When geniuses speak (or tweet), we listen. Here are the B2B influencers who make us drop everything we're doing whenever they post something new.

ARDATH ALBEE, Founder and CEO of Marketing Interactions

SCOTT BRINKER, Vice President of Platform Ecosystem, HubSpot

SEAN CALLAHAN, Content Team, LinkedIn Marketing Solutions

STEVE CASEY, Principal Analyst, Forrester

JUSTIN GRAY, Founder and CEO, LeadMD

ANN HANDLEY, Chief Content Officer, MarketingProfs

MATT HEINZ, President, Heinz Marketing

MEGAN HEUER, Vice President of Research, Sirius Decisions

CARLOS HIDALGO, Founder and CEO, VisumCX

PETER ISAACSON, CMO, Demandbase

DOUG KESSLER, Creative Director and Co-Founder, Velocity Partners

DAVID LEWIS, Founder and CEO, DemandGen International

KATIE MARTELL, Executive Director, Boston Content; on-demand consultant

JON MILLER, CEO of Engagio; previously co-founder and CMO of Marketo, an Adobe company

LEE ODDEN, CEO and Co-founder TopRank Marketing

DAVID RAAB, Principal, Raab Associates

LAURA RAMOS, Vice President and Principal Analyst, Forrester

MICHAEL ROSE, Mojo Media Labs

CRAIG ROSENBERG, Co-founder and Chief Analyst, TOPO

JILL ROWLEY, Partner, Stage 2 Capital

MATT SENATORE, Service Director of Account-Based Marketing, Sirius Decisions

SAMANTHA STONE, Founder and CMO, The Marketing Advisory Network

SCOTT SWEENEY, CEO, Mass MarTech

MATHEW SWEEZEY, Principal of Marketing Insights, Salesforce

ERIC WITTLAKE, Sr. Analyst, TOPO

Now you're officially ready for a B2B transformation.

The best action you can take is to start somewhere, and start today. Don't let anything stand in your way!

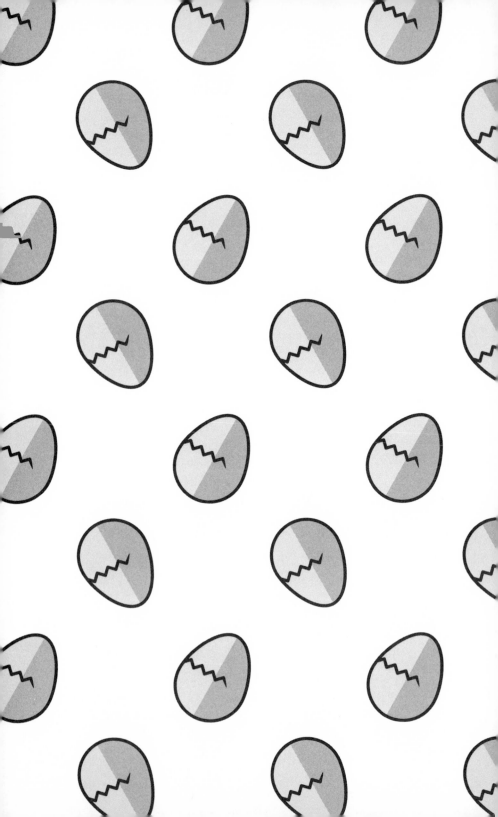

THE INNOVATIVE STORY
OF NEW STORY

New Story is an innovative nonprofit founded in 2015 that pioneers solutions to end global homelessness. Inspired to act after a trip to Haiti in 2013, CEO and Co-Founder Brett Hagler saw an opportunity to work with technology and transparency to challenge traditional methods of helping families meet their basic need for shelter.

New Story builds communities of $6,000-$10,000 homes in partnership with families living in extreme poverty. In four years, the nonprofit has funded over 2,300 homes, building 22 communities across Haiti, El Salvador, and Mexico and raising over $27 million to pioneer solutions through new software, processes, and homebuilding innovations.

In 2018, the organization partnered with ICON to create a first-of-its-kind machine and print the very first permitted, 3D-printed home in North America. This year, they're taking it even further, and 3D-printing an entire community. It's no surprise that Fast Company recognized New Story as one of the world's most innovative companies in 2017, and as a Top-10 nonprofit in 2019.

100% of the donations to New Story go directly toward building communities. That includes the proceeds from this book. We thank you for helping make dreams come true for deserving families.

About Brett Hagler, CEO & Co-Founder, New Story:

Brett is a Y Combinator alum, 2016 Forbes 30 Under 30 Entrepreneur, author, speaker, and cancer survivor. He lives by the mantra "It's only crazy until it's not," which is how he was able to go from starting a nonprofit at age 25 by building just one house to bringing breakthrough technologies to entire communities.

You can learn more about New Story at https://newstorycharity.org/

P.S. For every review of the book (good/bad), we will put $10 toward this charity.

So don't forget to write a review of the book!

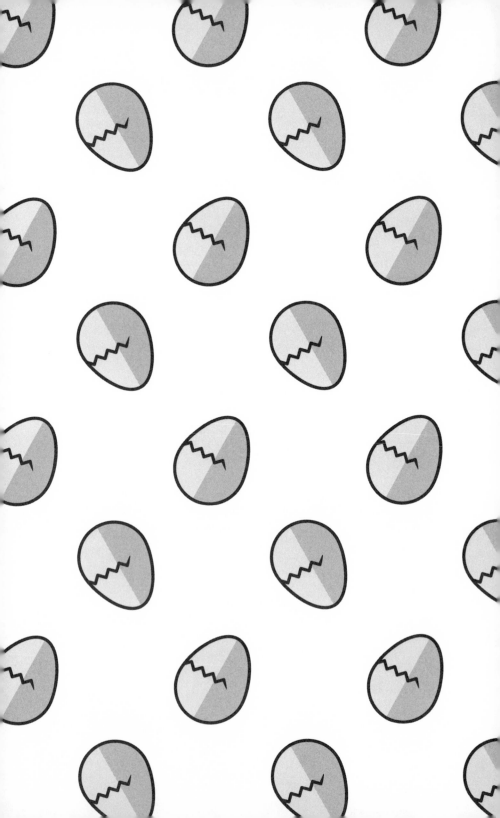

ACKNOWLEDGMENTS

We are incredibly grateful to countless people who have helped shape the content of this book. We thank you for your time and insights, which have made this book come to life.

Book reviewers and contributors:

Stuart English, Caitlin Burge, Chris Reene, Ryan Vitello, Alex Lawrence, Christina Simms, Jack McGlinchey, Sunny Bradshaw, Nicole Morrison, Jeff Campbell, Bryan Brown, Shea Castle, Stephanie Kelly, Brenna Zenaty, Janet Tambasco, Torrey Dye, Shannel Wheeler, Laura Galante, Clair Li, Kristin Hedge, Cathy Chandler, David Pyrzenski, Mark Jauregui, Todd Mccormick, Tim Kopp, Kelly Ford, Barb McGivern, Tracy Bolton, Jillian Gartner, Kristen Elton, Jamie Pasculli, Caroline Hareid, Colleen Jackson, April Meyer, Kalen Gordon, Mary Williams, Omar-Al-Sinjari, Malachi Threadgill, Daniel Englebretson, Jeremy Middleton, Julia Stead, Eric Martin, Justin Keller, Mark Stouse, Jill Rowley, Trish Bertuzzi, Andrew Gaffney, James Carbary, Samantha Stone, Steve Watt, Ethan Beaute, Trish Agarwal, Jay Baer, Scott Brinker, Meagen Eisenberg, Corinne Sklar, Justin Keller, Carlos Hidalgo, Mike Rose and Nikole Rose, Michael Ziman, Baillie Ward and Erin Moeller.

And the entire Terminus team and the FlipMyFunnel community for helping make this book possible!

ABM IS B2B.

28 most common acronyms, terms, and phrases you should know:

As this concept of "ABM is B2B." or #ABMisB2B gains popularity, it seems that there are a number of new terms came along with it. If you're relatively new to account-based marketing, you may find yourself overwhelmed by all the acronyms, terms, and phrases that are thrown around.

To get you up to speed on account-based lingo, we've compiled a glossary of common ABM terms you need to know before you launch your own ABM program.

ACCOUNT-BASED MARKETING (ABM)

Account-based marketing is an end-to-end go-to-market strategy designed to focus a majority of marketing, sales, and success effort on the pre- and post-sales accounts with the highest likelihood of closing, through data-driven targeting and personalization programs at scale.

Put simply, it's a much more targeted, personalized, and proactive marketing strategy that focuses on your best-fit accounts.

ACCOUNT INTELLIGENCE

Account intelligence is the overall knowledge you have of a target account, meaning you understand who they are and what they really want and need. It goes deeper than top-level insights and often requires the assistance of third-party data providers.

Gathering account intelligence typically involves a four-pronged approach of Fit, Intent, Relationship, and Engagement (FIRE) data, which will be outlined in more detail later on.

When marketing campaigns are built with limited intelligence about the target account, you typically fail to strike the target.

ACCOUNT LIFECYCLE

The account lifecycle is the ABM version of the buyer's journey. And while the buyer's journey (Awareness, Consideration, Decision) is very lead-focused (with a focus on the individual), account lifecycles take into consideration the entire buying committee. It includes three overarching phases: Acquisition, Acceleration, and Expansion. Within those phases are seven distinct stages:

- **The Acquisition Phase:** efforts made to bring net-new accounts into the pipeline with the goal of driving meaningful engagement
  - Pre-Targeting
  - Account Nurture

- **The Acceleration Phase:** accelerating the engaged accounts in your pipeline or re-engaging cold opportunities to bring them back to life and ultimately close deals
  - Pipeline Acceleration
  - Dead Opportunity Win-Back

- **The Expansion Phase:** directing resources toward increasing customer retention rates, expanding opportunities with those customers and exploring cross-selling and upselling opportunities when it's time for them to renew
  - Retention
  - Cross-Sell and Upsell
  - Land and Expand

ABM *is* **B2B.**

ACCOUNT TIERING

Account tiering is a common practice that refers to the process of segmenting your target account list based on priority and revenue opportunity. Tiering your accounts involves using technology, data points, and good old-fashioned research to prioritize your dream accounts.

Typically, account-based marketers leverage a three-tier system:

- Tier 1 accounts are perfect ICP* fits, similar to your highest value customers. Tier 1 also includes logos with strategic value or accounts that show high fit, intent, and/or engagement.
- Tier 2 accounts are strong ICP fits but have a lower lifetime value.
- Tier 3 accounts fit most, but not all, ICP criteria. They're worth pursuing but typically not worth investing significant resources to win their business (either because they don't match the ICP criteria or they're not showing intent or engagement).

AVERAGE CONTRACT VALUE (ACV)

This one is pretty self-explanatory – your ACV is the average annualized revenue per customer contract.

BUYER PERSONA

Buyer personas are overviews of the people you engage with directly during the sales process. They are used to guide your sales, marketing, and customer success teams throughout the buyer and customer lifecycle. Think of a buyer persona as a "composite sketch" of your customers.

Unlike traditional lead-based advertising, in account-based marketing, you don't need to focus as much on the minutiae of the individual person's character traits. Instead, you need to focus more on their buying habits.

Many argue that buyer personas are rendered obsolete in ABM, but that's not the case – while your Ideal Customer Profile (ICP) is crucial, your buyer personas help to support the messaging you're distributing to the accounts that fall into your ICP. After all, everyone brings a different perspective to their account lifecycle, and it's important that you're aware of who you're marketing to in your accounts.

COOKIE TARGETING

Cookie-based targeting allows you to serve personalized ads to different personas (think job title or department) within a target account by serving ads based on cookie data. Unlike retargeting ads, which require a person to visit a page on your company's website, Terminus is able to collect cookie data on target accounts before they ever visit your site – this is what we call proactive targeting, and helps you stay one step ahead of the competition.

ENGAGEMENT DATA

Engagement is any interaction that a person – known or unknown – has with your company, online or offline. Engagement data, therefore, is a measure of this level of interaction.

However, different companies measure engagement in different ways – it can be hard to quantify quality vs. poor engagement, so we recommend defining what meaningful engagement means in your organization before you start measuring and making decisions based on account engagement.

Here's what a simplified layered model for meaningful engagement might look:

# of total website visits from # people +

# of visits to high-value webpages from # people +

# of content downloads from # people +

# of email opens from # people

FIRMOGRAPHIC

Firmographics are the attributes account-based marketers (and B2B companies in general) use to segment their target market in order to discover their ideal consumers.

Common firmographics include:

- Industry

- Revenue

- Company Size

- Geography/Location

- Account Lifecycle Stage

FIT DATA

Fit data, again, is pretty self-explanatory – it's a measure of how well a company "fits" your ICP. Fit data relies on advanced firmographics technology used, recent founding, and conferences attended by employees. Leveraging advanced firmographics to measure fit enables you to get way more targeted with your marketing and sales campaigns.

F.I.R.E

FIRE is an acronym that refers to the four-pronged model of ABM success:

- **Fit:** knowing your target accounts

- **Intent:** knowing which of your target accounts are actively researching or buying your product/solution so you can prioritize these accounts

- **Relationship:** knowing which accounts have the deepest relationship with your company

- **Engagement:** creating engagement with the right people in the right accounts

IDEAL CUSTOMER PROFILE (ICP)

An ideal customer profile is a description of the company — not the individual buyer or end user — that's a perfect fit for your solution.

Your ICP should focus on relevant characteristics of your target accounts, such as:

- Industry/vertical
- Employee headcount — companywide and within key departments
- Annual revenue
- Budget
- Geography
- Technology they use
- Size of their customer base
- Level of organizational or technological maturity

INTENT DATA

Intent data shows you what companies are researching on third-party sites, not your sites. Intent signals help your sales team determine what an account is interested in before they come to your website, giving them the visibility they need to tailor their strategies and further personalize their outreach.

Intent data relies on third-party data from platforms like Bombora or G2Crowd.

IP TARGETING

IP targeting is based on the actual physical address of where a company is located. An IP address (Internet Protocol address) is the unique numerical label assigned to every device that communicates on a computer network within an organization.

While cookie-based targeting helps you get more granular with your targeting, IP targeting can help you get in front of more people worldwide (as many countries prevent marketers from leveraging cookie data in their targeting because of GDPR regulations).

LAND AND EXPAND

"Land and Expand" is a sales strategy in which you close a small deal with a target account and then work to sell upsell or cross-sell within the organization to gain more traction and revenue.

MARKETING QUALIFIED ACCOUNT

A marketing qualified account (MQA) is the ABM equivalent of a marketing qualified lead. Just as an MQL is marked as "ready to pass on to sales", an MQA is an account that's shown a high enough level of engagement to indicate possible sales readiness.

OUTBOUND MARKETING

Outbound marketing is a more proactive marketing strategy in which a company initiates (or attempts to initiate) the discussion with a target account instead of waiting for a contact in a target account to raise their hand (via traditional inbound methods, like a form fill).

PIPELINE ACCELERATION

Pipeline acceleration (as a goal) is the act of increasing the speed at which an account moves through the account lifecycle. This typically involves an acceleration campaign, where marketing and sales work together to move accounts through the sales process.

PLAY

An ABM play is a defined set of steps that marketing and sales will do when an account does a specific action. This action triggers the execution of any goal-oriented activity – for example, when an account shows an increase in engagement, a marketing team will create a one-to-one ad for that company and the sales rep will send a piece of direct mail.

RELATIONSHIP DATA

Relationship data is the means of identifying and quantifying the entire network of relationships that your employees have within an account.

Relationship data helps you gain insight into the quality of relationships and engagement within your target accounts.

TACTIC

The formal definition of tactic is, "an action or strategy carefully planned to achieve a specific end". Within the context of ABM, a tactic is basically a strategy you use within a marketing campaign. Tactics help you reach and engage their target companies and expand your funnel.

An example of a tactic might be:

- A piece of direct mail
- A nurturing email
- A new eBook

Mentioning/interacting with target accounts on social media

TARGET ACCOUNT LIST (TAL)

Whereas your Total Addressable Market (TAM) is all the accounts you could sell to, your Target Account List (TAL) is a list of all accounts you want to sell to right now. You can build out a list of your target accounts using the FIRE (Fit, Intent, Relationship, Engagement) data we've defined above.

T.E.A.M

TEAM is framework Terminus uses and advocates everyone to use to execute their ABM programs. It's a comprehensive framework that drives successful, account-centric programs where marketing & sales act as a unified team.

The TEAM framework addresses the core functional areas of a modern B2B marketing organization: targeting, engagement, activation, and measurement.

Here's how each fits into a successful ABM strategy:

- **Target:** Align and operationalize marketing and sales efforts around a unified target account strategy
- **Engage:** Create and orchestrate programs and campaigns with your ideal customers
- **Activate:** Alert and enable sales when their accounts show intent or engagement to win more deals by using account level engagement data and AI
- **Measure:** Prove the success of your ABM program, see how ABM is driving pipeline, revenue, velocity, and deal size for all of your account lists

TECHNOGRAPHIC

At its most basic, technographic data are insights into the technology an organization or its employees use – otherwise known as their tech stack.

TOTAL ADDRESSABLE MARKET (TAM)

Your Total Addressable Market is the total available opportunity for your product or services – essentially, it's everyone you could sell to.

The basic calculation for your TAM:

average revenue * number of customers for the entire segment of the targeted market

Now that you've got a solid grasp on some of the most common "ABM to B2B" terms, you can start diving into more technical material and find ways to design, launch, and maintain your own amazing B2B campaigns.

ABM *is* **B2B.**

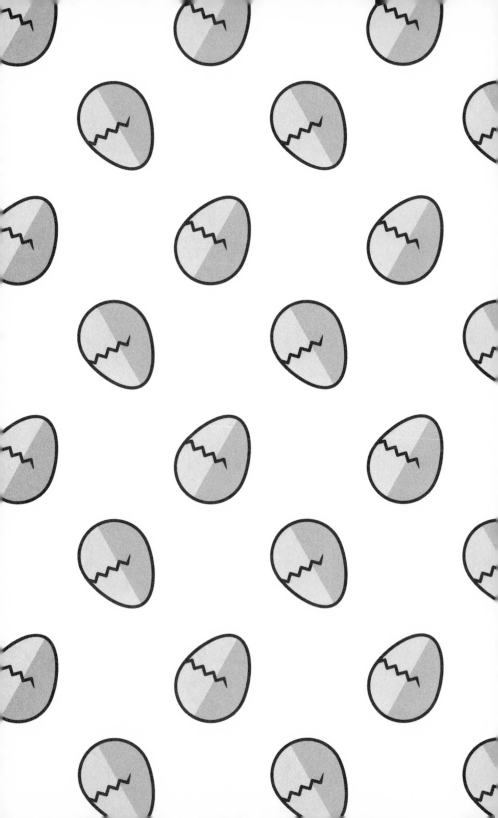

INDEX